MANHATTAN ON FILM 2

More Walking Tours of Location Sites in The Big Apple

Manhattan on Film 2

More Walking Tours of Location Sites in the Big Apple

Chuck Katz

Limelight Editions

MANHATTAN ON FILM 2

First Limelight Edition, October 2002

 Published by Proscenium Publishers Inc., New York.

Manufactured in the United States of America.

Interior design by Mulberry Tree Press, Inc.
(MulberryTreePress.com)

Library of Congress Cataloging-in-Publication Data
Katz, Chuck.
Manhattan on film 2 : more walking tours of location sites in the Big Apple / by Chuck Katz.--
1st Limelight ed.
p. cm.
Includes index.
ISBN 0-87910-975-0

1. Motion picture locations--New York (State)--New York--Guidebooks. 2. Manhattan (New York, N.Y.)--Guidebooks. I. Title: Manhattan on film two. II. Title.
PN1995.67.N7 K383 2002
384'.8'097471--dc21

2002012548

To Ashley
For being at my side

To Jaden
For coming into our lives

To Dad
For always being there

To Mom
For watching from above

Acknowledgments

So many people have lent their support during the past year (when I first started working on *Manhattan on Film 2*) that it is hard to mention names without fearing I will leave someone out. Nevertheless, life is about taking risks, so here I go . . . My heartfelt thanks to the following: Dad, who is once again going strong, for hanging in there and all the while redefining the word "support"; Phyllis, for coming along when she did—like the cavalry appearing in the classic westerns when all seems lost—and for caring as much as she does; Jim, for being there through some difficult times and for helping me sort through a mountain of stills in search of just the right ones for this book; Jeff and Dave, for remembering that every family has its good times and bad, and the best families hang in there together; Ryan O'Neal, for threatening to ban me from his gym if I didn't include the immortal *Love* Story in this volume; Bill Loafman, Jeannette Bond, Alex Deland and Jackson Browning (no, not the guy who sings "Late for the Sky") for remembering that my skills extend beyond the identification and description of movie sites (not to minimize such skills, of course); Duane Morris, for giving me a reason to put on a jacket and tie and for having the faith that I will meet their expectations; Lisa Soeder and Michela Daliana, for redefining what it is to be a friend; Alejandro, Bill, Blumkin, Churn, Doug, Michael, Ken, Labo, Paul, Ray, Scott and Tom, and others I may have accidentally omitted, for making up an All-Star roster of good friends; Captain Dave McCarthy, for answering the call of duty and heading overseas to protect our way of life against the cowardly terrorists; Debbie Lang, for pounding the pavement to get my screenplays and television scripts read by the powers that be; Mel, for believing once more in the concept of *Manhattan on Film*; the 92nd St. Y, for letting me lead my walking tours and ask my silly trivia questions along the way; Jaden, for reminding me, every day since September 11, that this world can still produce miracles; and my dearest Ashley, for agreeing to travel down the road of life with me, through the best of times and the worst of times.

Contents

Preface

In the preface to *Manhattan on Film: Walking Tours of Hollywood's Fabled Front Lot* (Limelight Editions 1999), I explained how I came up with the idea of putting together a book of movie locations. I will not bore you with a repeat of my reasoning here, but urge you to go out and get *Manhattan on Film.*

A large number of movies were intentionally excluded from *Manhattan on Film*, so as to keep it portable and user-friendly. And although *Manhattan on Film 2: More Walking Tours of Location Sites in the Big Apple* stands on its own as a guide to movie locations, completely separate and independent from *Manhattan on Film*, the two books are intended to be companion pieces and together, should give a vast and thorough history of Manhattan's role in movies during the past three-quarters of a century.

In a very few instances, I have referred to locations covered in *Manhattan on Film*, but only in those rare cases where I felt it necessary to draw the TourWalker's attention to something that had been covered in that first volume. But there is something from *Manhattan on Film* that recent events compel me to mention here. In the preface to *Manhattan on Film*, I cautioned that although I intended to limit the book to locations "still in existence," there would always be some locations, like restaurants and stores, which "close and reopen almost overnight." But I went on to say that certain locations, such as the Empire State Building, were "presumably here to stay."

I began writing this preface two weeks after the horrific and cowardly acts of unthinkable and godless terrorism that destroyed thousands of lives and eradicated the World Trade Center from existence, and immediately realized how naïve and wrong I was, and how vulnerable and short-lived any man-made structures have the potential to be. In my years practicing public finance law, I have been to offices in the World Trade Center dozens and dozens of time, often spending late nights trying to get deals closed. I have eaten in the restaurants at the top and shopped in the stores in the ground level Concourse. I had friends in those buildings: Some are now gone and some must now carry on in a much different place in a vastly changed world.

I wavered as to what to do when **Walking Tour 13: America's Heart** got to the former site of the World Trade Center, because, as you might imagine, there were certainly a few movies that situated scenes in what has been one of the most recognizable structures on this Planet Earth. As you will see, I have decided to include those locations and those movies, as a tribute to the people who lost their lives during the tragedy that struck New York on September 11, 2001. To do otherwise would have risked sending a signal to terrorists that they had won, that with two indescribably heinous acts, they had succeeded in eradicating not only the structures, but also the people who had brought them to life and the memory of what they had stood for. And that was for me something almost as unthinkable as the acts themselves.

So **Walking Tour 13: America's Heart** will sadly and reverently, yet proudly, mention the movies that had scenes filmed at the World Trade Center, in hopes that we remember the good that there continues to be in this world, and that we never forget the evil that we must fight against on an almost daily basis.

With that said, there are a few basics to remember as you follow this book to nearly 300 locations in Manhattan. Each Tour is set up by neighborhood and is intended to take no more than two hours, although the duration depends as much on your pace as on the amount of ground covered. Naturally, each Tour is best enjoyed on foot.

How you get to the starting point is up to you, but I have done my best to start each Tour as close as possible to a bus and/or subway stop and have identified the means of mass transit that can get you to there. Buses should be exited at the nearest stop to the one indicated. The subway and bus systems in New York City are always fluid, but even more so after the World Trade Center attacks. I have done my best to reflect subway and bus routes as they exist today, but there is no guarantee that service on particular lines will not be suspended, re-routed or discontinued (especially on the lines that run downtown on Manhattan's west side). Always consult the most recent subway and bus maps before attempting to use mass transit in Manhattan.

The focus of *Manhattan on Film 2* is exteriors. Thus, when I point out a building and indicate it is where a particular character lived (*e.g.*, Pierce Brosnan (a.k.a. Thomas Crown) in *The Thomas Crown Affair*), I do not mean to suggest that any of the movie's interior scenes were filmed there. In addition, these Tours do not require you to enter a building, although some of the buildings are open to the public and it is entirely up to you whether to go inside or not.

As was the case with *Manhattan on Film*, it is strongly suggested that all Walking Tours be followed during daylight hours. The locations are easier to find and easier to appreciate during the day, and it is never a good idea to walk around at night with your nose in a book.

As I often refer to a location in terms of direction (*e.g.*, northeast corner of a particular intersection, or west side of a particular avenue), it will be necessary for the TourWalker to understand these directional references. The City's "compass" is easier to grasp than you might imagine. For example, coming uptown and standing at the intersection of Third Avenue and 68th Street, you will find that 69th Street is ahead of you, north of 68th (while 67th is behind you and south) and Second Avenue is to your right, east of Third (while Lexington Avenue is to your left, west). If you are unsure of the directionals, consult the map at the start of each Walking Tour or simply ask one of the friendly New Yorkers walking by. They will be only too happy to help.

In my descriptions of the scenes from a movie filmed at a certain location, I have tried to be a little more creative than simply describing a scene and saying which movie it was in. Throughout the book, titles of all movies are shown in *italics*, so there should be no confusion as to what is being discussed at each particular location.

Finally, I sincerely hope that you enjoy taking these tours as much as I enjoyed putting them together.

Chuck Katz
July 2002

Manhattan on Film 2

More Walking Tours of Location Sites in The Big Apple

BABE IN TOYL
F·A·O SCHWARZ
FIFTH AVENUE
EXIT ONLY

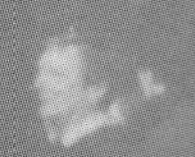

Walking Tour 1

The Plaza and Its Neighbors

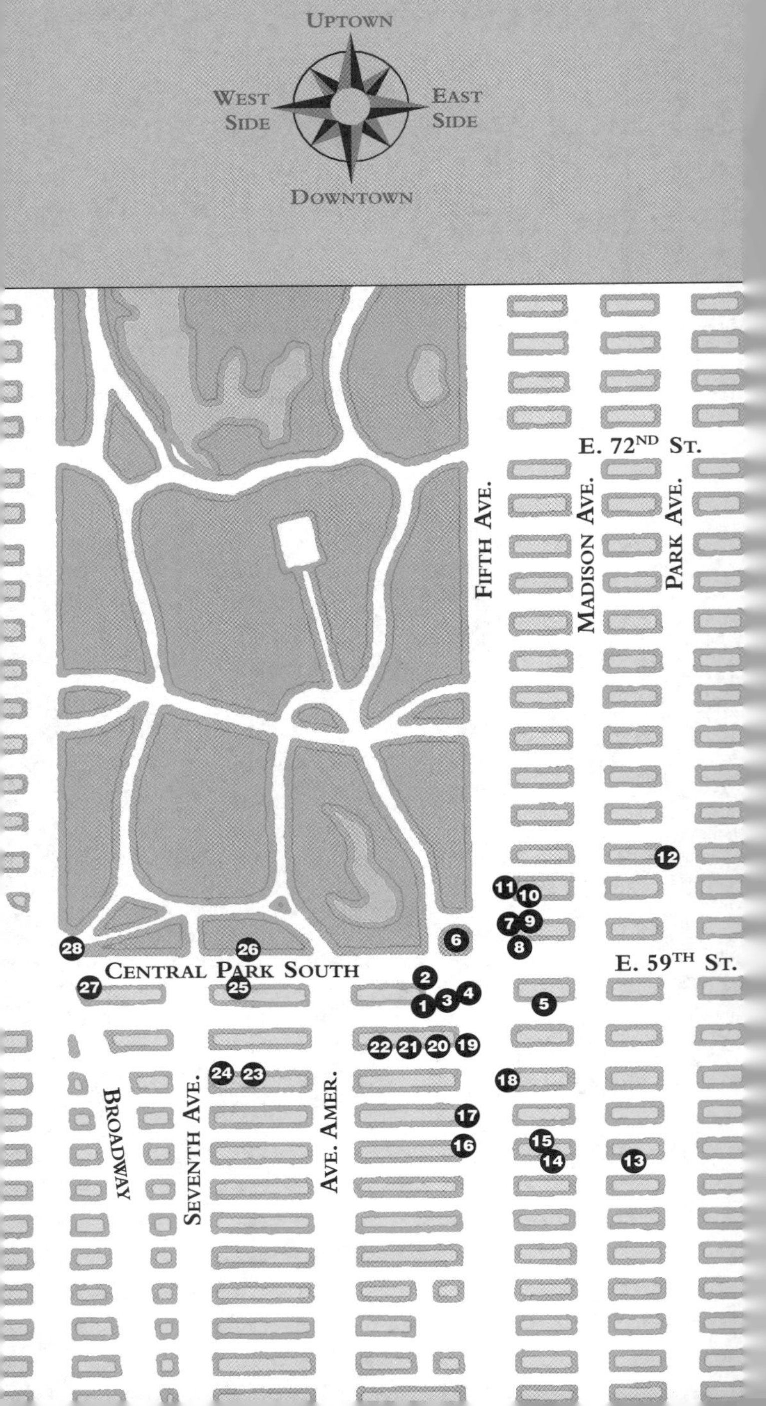

E. 72ND ST.

FIFTH AVE.

MADISON AVE.

PARK AVE.

12

11 10

7 9

6

8

28

26

CENTRAL PARK SOUTH

E. 59TH ST.

2

27

25

1 3 4

5

22 21 20 19

24 23

18

BROADWAY

SEVENTH AVE.

AVE. AMER.

17

16

15

14

13

Walking Tour 1

The Plaza and Its Neighbors

In the movies, when out-of-towners come to New York, there is a good chance they will stay at the Plaza Hotel. It has appeared in so many films, it is probably the unofficial hotel for the well-to-do who come to the Big Apple, whether on business or vacation. But The Plaza goes far beyond the comforts and luxuries offered within its doors. It also sits near some of the best locations in some of New York's most memorable films.

Walking Tour 1: The Plaza and its Neighbors begins at the southeast corner of Central Park, at the intersection of 59th Street (Central Park South) and Fifth Avenue. If you choose to get to the starting point by public transportation, you may use any of the following subway or bus lines (although the following list is by no means exhaustive):

FROM THE NORTH

SUBWAYS

- **4, 5 or 6** southbound to 59th Street. Walk west on 59th to Fifth Avenue.

BUSES

- **M1, M2, M3 or M4** southbound on Fifth Avenue to 59th Street.

FROM THE SOUTH

SUBWAYS

- **4, 5** or **6** northbound to 59th Street. Walk west on 59th to Fifth Avenue.

- **N** or **R** northbound to 59th Street, just west of Fifth Avenue. Walk east on 59th to Fifth.
- **Q** or **W** northbound to 59th Street, just west of Fifth Avenue. Walk east on 59th to Fifth.

BUSES

- **M1, M2, M3** or **M4** northbound on Madison Avenue to 59th Street. Walk west on 59th to Fifth.
- **M5, M6** or **M7** northbound on Avenue of the Americas to 59th Street. Walk east on 59th to Fifth.

FROM THE EAST

BUSES

- **M31** southbound on York Avenue to 57th Street, then westbound on 57th to Fifth Avenue. Walk north on Fifth to 59th Street.
- **M57** westbound on 57th Street to Fifth Avenue. Walk north on Fifth to 59th Street.

FROM THE WEST

SUBWAYS

- **1, 2, B** or **C** southbound to 59th Street/Columbus Circle. Walk east on 59th to Fifth Avenue.

BUSES

- **M5** southbound on Riverside Drive, then Broadway, then eastbound on 59th Street to Fifth Avenue.
- **M7** southbound on Columbus Avenue, then Broadway, then eastbound on 59th Street to Seventh Avenue. Walk east on 59th to Fifth Avenue.
- **M104** southbound on Broadway to Columbus Circle. Walk east on 59th to Fifth Avenue.

If you are not already there, cross to the west side of Fifth Avenue and enjoy an unobstructed view of the Plaza Hotel, which stands grandly before the southeast entrance to Central Park.

1. The Plaza Hotel. 59th Street, west of Fifth Avenue. From musicals to dramas, comedies to thrillers, The Plaza has seen it all. His movie career on the wane, Tony Hunter (Fred Astaire) decided to try his hand on the Broadway stage. His co-star was ballerina Gabrielle Girard (Cyd Charisse), but they couldn't have irritated each other more. And then, one evening, they left the hotel, hopped on a horse-drawn carriage, and went for an enchanting ride around the City. After that, the success of their collaboration was all but assured, both onscreen and off, as depicted in *The Band Wagon*.

Janice Courtney (Debbie Reynolds) was being worked to the bone and running on all cylinders, but she kept on going. But when she collapsed during a photo session inside her hotel room in *My Six Loves*, her doctor prescribed six weeks of uninterrupted rest and Janice headed to the country. It was there that she learned there was more to life than work.

Not only did Neil Simon set one of his movies here, he incorporated the name into the title. In *Plaza Suite*, three different stories, starring Walter Matthau, Maureen Stapleton and Lee Grant, among others, played out inside this hotel.

In *Love at First Bite*, Count Dracula (George Hamilton) also stayed at this hotel. But unlike most guests, who used their rooms primarily at night, the Count preferred to spend his evening hours out on the town, catching up on his sleep during the day.

Having already been told by producer Arnold Kreplich (Alan King)

that movie star Alice Detroit (Dyan Cannon) had agreed to do his play, playwright Ivan Travalian (Al Pacino) was surprised to learn that there was still one small detail that he and Arnold had to take care of: go ask Alice. Less than pleased with Arnold's little white lie, Ivan accompanied him when they met the star at the Palm Court in the Plaza's lobby and got her to agree to sign on, in *Author! Author!*

Hailing from a small town, just in from the airport and mistaken for a pair of twins, one identical to each of them, Sadie (Better Midler) and Rose (Lily Tomlin) Ratliff were dropped off here by a limousine and shown to their room. Well, not exactly their room. A few minutes later, their other halves, Sadie (Better Midler) and Rose (Lily Tomlin) Shelton, who were bigwigs in *Big Business*, showed up and were given a room adjacent to the one occupied by the Sisters Ratliff. With two sets of twins in the hotel, havoc was sure to follow. And it did.

They were young, but having grown up in New York, they acted like adults. Dressed in their best formal attire, the group of friends in *Metropolitan* spent a good deal of the Christmas season gathering here, in the ornate splendor of one of the rooms, talking and acting mature.

He was growing up fast and living a life he could hardly have imagined, but it had its seamier side, too. In *Almost Famous*, underage "Rolling Stone" reporter William Miller (Patrick Fugit) had followed the band Stillwater around on its tour, which culminated here in New York. But when he found Penny Lane (Kate Hudson) in a room in this hotel, having overdosed as a way of dealing with the pain of losing rock star Russell (Billy Crudup) to his wife, William was forced to grow up even more.

If you would like to go inside The Plaza and

have a drink at the Oak Room, go ahead. But be careful . . .

2. Oak Room in the Plaza Hotel. While having a drink in the Oak Room, advertising executive Roger Thornhill (Cary Grant) innocently went to send a wire and was mistaken for a man named George Kaplan. He was ushered (at gunpoint) into a car waiting out in the street and whisked away to an estate on Long Island, in *North By Northwest*. Thornhill eventually made his escape and his way back to the hotel, to learn more about the mysterious George Kaplan.

Out in front of the steps leading to the Plaza's elegant front door, you should see doormen and guests coming and going. The perfect place to get your point across to the passersby.

3. In Front of The Plaza Hotel. Ever the political activist, Katie (Barbra Streisand) handed out leaflets for the American Soviet Benefit in front of the hotel. Years later, with a lot of turbulent water under the bridge, Katie ran into her lifelong love, Hubbell Gardner (Robert

Redford), on the same spot. They had parted ways long before and were no longer a couple, but their eyes told a different story, in *The Way We Were*.

Take a look at the fountain in front of The Plaza.

4. Plaza Hotel Fountain. He was unhappily married to Mary (Joanne Woodward), a very cold woman, ironically, his wife in real life. But he realized that he would rather be happy with someone else than miserable with his wife, so Alfred (Paul Newman), in *From the Terrace*, arranged a late-night rendezvous by this fountain with Natalie (Ina Balin).

While Alfred learned after he got married that his wife was not the one for him, another man sensed on the eve of his wedding that he was destined to be with someone else. Not willing to leave things entirely to chance, Jonathan Trager (John Cusack) took the initiative and cancelled his wedding on the very morning he was to walk down the aisle. Afterwards, not certain if he had done the right thing, Jonathan walked near this fountain with best friend Dean Kansky (Jeremy Piven). Dean was supportive of his friend's actions, realizing after his own marriage had broken apart that sometimes it is necessary to act, and other times it is okay to rely on *Serendipity*.

Before going anywhere, turn and look at F.A.O. Schwarz, directly across Fifth Avenue.

5. F.A.O. Schwarz. 767 Fifth Avenue (at 58th Street). On her first trip to the big city in *Big Business*, Sadie Ratliff (Bette Midler) went on a window-shopping spree that brought her to this world famous toy emporium. There she was spotted by Jason (Seth Green), who mistook her for his mother, Sadie Shelton (also Bette Midler), and tried out his toy boxing gloves on her. It took them a long time to finally figure out who was who, but not before they had all endured a great deal of confusion and mayhem.

A number of years before, while his colleague, Arthur (Blaine Novak) kept her son occupied, undercover sleuth John (Ben Gazzara) initiated contact with the subject of his surveillance, Angela (Audrey Hepburn) while she was shopping in the store. The movie was *They All Laughed* and at the time, the store was located across 58th Street from its current location.

Now turn left and head north on Fifth Avenue. Cross 59th Street (Central Park South) to the north side of the street. The small block you are on is known as Grand Army Plaza.

6. Fifth Avenue between 59th and 60th Streets. Grand Army Plaza. While under surveillance by the police, who hoped he would lead them to their quarry, Alvin Sanders (Jamie Foxx) answered a ringing phone on this little plot of land and was told the man he was supposed to meet was sitting on one of the benches on the plaza. But as the cops swarmed the area, cordoned off the small plaza and swooped in on their prey, they discovered they had surrounded the wrong man, and realized that Alvin may have set them up, in retaliation for their having used him as *Bait*.

Now, look across Fifth Avenue.

7. Sherry Netherland Hotel. 781 Fifth Avenue. Detective Danny Madigan (Richard Widmark) came to meet his wife Julia (Inger Stevens) in Suite 1004 of this hotel before escorting her to the Captains' Association Dinner Dance, in *Madigan*.

8. Harry Cipriani, in the Sherry Netherland Hotel. After meeting at a fundraiser the night before, insurance investigator Catherine Banning (Rene Russo) and billionaire industrialist Thomas Crown (Pierce Brosnan) came here for dinner, in *The Thomas Crown Affair*. But her intentions were not pure. While Catherine kept Crown occupied, the police made copies of his house keys, which Catherine had swiped from him, and searched his home for evidence linking him to a brazen art theft. But, as always, Crown was one step ahead of them all.

Continue north along Fifth Avenue until you reach 60th Street. Cross Fifth Avenue and stand on the southeast corner of Fifth Avenue and 60th.

9. Fifth Avenue and 60th Street. Southeast Corner. In a building on this corner, in *Tales of Manhattan*, actor Paul Allman (Charles Boyer) waited patiently for a tailcoat to be delivered to his apartment. With much fanfare, the coat was delivered and placed on a mannequin in Allman's home. He didn't seem concerned when he learned the tailcoat was supposedly cursed. But perhaps he should have been.

Head east on 60th Street a very short distance

until you are across from the ornate façade of the Metropolitan Club at 1 East 60th Street.

10. The Metropolitan Club. 1 East 60th Street. Having just moved to New York, Finn (Ethan Hawke) was thrilled to run into his long-term friend and childhood crush, Estella (Gwyneth Paltrow). And he was even more excited when she invited him to join her and her friends for a drink here, fueling his *Great Expectations*. But he left, deflated, having learned that Estella was dating Walter (Hank Azaria) and seemed to view Finn as nothing more than an old friend. So distraught that he left with a jacket the Club had given him to wear while inside, Finn had to return the jacket in front of these gates, where a Club employee caught up with him.

Return to Fifth Avenue, turn right, cross 60th Street and walk north until you are in front of the Pierre Hotel.

11. The Pierre Hotel. Fifth Avenue (between 60th and 61st Streets). Weddings weren't supposed to be his thing, and he never imagined he would want to fall into such a trap himself, but when playboy Charlie Reader (Frank Sinatra) returned from Europe, he came here from the airport to attend a wedding. He arrived just in time to blow a kiss to the bride, catch the bouquet and realize that falling into a tender trap wouldn't be so bad, if the trap was the one set by Julie Gillis (Debbie Reynolds), in *The Tender Trap*.

Continue north the short distance to 61st Street. Turn right on 61st and walk east two blocks. Turn left on Park Avenue and walk north to the Regency Hotel, at 540 Park.

12. Regency Hotel. 540 Park Avenue (between 61st and 62nd Streets). Things weren't easy for Frankie (Ed Harris). His business operations were illicit and he had to deal with a bad seed like Terry (Sean Penn), who was dating his daughter Kathleen (Robin Wright). Frankie came to talk to Kathleen, who worked here, in hopes of convincing her to choose another guy, in *State of Grace*.

Head south on Park Avenue. At 54th Street, turn right and head west, stopping halfway between Park and Madison Avenues.

13. 54th Street, between Park and Madison Avenues. It was just before the start of the Thanksgiving holiday and in the search for available taxicabs, it was every man for himself, as Neal Page (Steve Martin) quickly learned, in *Planes, Trains and Automobiles*. Standing on the corner of 54th and Madison, Neal eyed one of those scarce resources just down 54th Street, toward Park Avenue. But on the other side of the street, another man (Kevin Bacon) spied the same cab and the race was on. Avoiding obstacles as if they were in a steeplechase race, the two men vied for the cab, but Neal tripped and fell into the street, right near where you are now standing. He was lucky he didn't get run over, but Kevin Bacon won the prize.

Continue west on 54th Street. Cross Madison Avenue and walk the very short distance until you are in front of 25 East 54th.

14. 25 East 54th Street (same as 532 Madison Avenue). Staking out a gift shop across the street (which is no longer there), Detective Buddy (Roy Scheider) stood just inside this doorway, waiting for the proper moment to strike, at the beginning of *The Seven-Ups*. After a few minutes, Buddy crossed the street, entered the store and the sting operation was commenced.

Return to Madison, turn left and walk north to 55th Street. Turn left on 55th and walk west until you are in front of Lespinasse, which is adjacent to the St. Regis Hotel.

15. Lespinasse. 2 East 55th Street. Hoping to convince beauty pageant consultant Victor Fleming (Michael Caine) to turn her into a bona fide contestant, F.B.I. agent Gracie Hart (Sandra Bullock) had lunch with Fleming here, in *Miss Congeniality*.

Continue west on 55th Street. At Fifth Avenue, stop and look diagonally across the intersection of Fifth and 55th, to the Peninsula Hotel.

16. The Peninsula Hotel. 700 Fifth Avenue (at 55th Street). One minute she was rooting on her beloved New York Knicks, the next she was plucked from obscurity to coach the team. A dream come true for any avid fan. But at a dinner here with the eccentric team owner, Wild Bill Burgess (Frank Langella), Eddie Franklin (Whoopi Goldberg) learned that Wild Bill intended to move New York's beloved basketball team to St. Louis. Willing to walk away from her dream, Eddie left the dinner and the hotel, and hailed a passing cab, in *Eddie*.

Turn right and walk north on Fifth until you are across from Henri Bendel, which is between 55th and 56th Streets.

17. Henri Bendel Store. 712 Fifth Avenue (between 55th and 56th Streets). After winning the lottery, Muriel (Rosie Perez) and husband Charlie (Nicolas Cage) went on a shopping spree to spend some of their newfound wealth. In *It Could Happen to You*, it happened to them, and this fashionable emporium was one of the many stops on their spree.

Continue north on Fifth and stop halfway between 56th and 57th Streets, directly in front of the main entrance to Trump Tower.

18. Fifth Avenue (between 56th and 57th Streets). In front of Trump Tower. Molly (Meryl Streep) and Isabelle (Dianne Wiest) worked in New York and often walked in front of Trump Tower, here on Fifth Avenue. And when they walked, they talked. They discussed work, their respective relationships and their lives. But one thing Molly didn't discuss with Isabelle was the fact that, though married, she was *Falling in Love*, with Frank (Robert De Niro).

Continue north on Fifth and cross to the far side of 57th Street. Turn left and cross Fifth Avenue. Bergdorf-Goodman should loom before you, slightly to your right.

19. Bergdorf-Goodman. 754 Fifth Avenue. After agreeing to accompany Phillip Shane (Cary Grant) to Bermuda, and thereafter on a trip around the world, the less-than-worldly Cathy Timberlake (Doris Day) first had to get some new clothes. With Mr. Shane picking up the tab, in this the cinematic predecessor to Julia Roberts' shopping spree in *Pretty Woman*, Cathy came here in *That Touch of Mink*, tried on a vast array of clothes and left with a whole new wardrobe.

Turn left and walk west on 57th Street. Stop at 7 West 57th, which is the building just east of the big red "9."

20. 7 West 57th Street. After unleashing her wild side while on vacation in Greece, Ann (Liv Ullman) returned to her normal existence, which included working in a real estate office, located in this building. But when Peter (Edward Albert), her vacation "fling" surfaced in New York, Ann found that it might not be so easy to return to the life she had known before. For Ann's life in *40 Carats*, that turned out not to be such a bad thing.

Walk the short distance until you are in front of 9 West 57th Street (the building with the large red "9" out front).

21. 9 West 57th Street. In *Superman*, a burglar improbably scaled the front of this building. As he made his way up, he had planned for everything except the possibility that he might find Superman (Christopher Reeve) standing in his path, throwing a wrench in his plans. Startled, the burglar fell, but luckily Superman was quick to catch him before he hit the ground.

Continue heading west on 57th Street and stop in front of Rizzoli Books, at 31 West 57th.

22. Rizzoli Books. 31 West 57th Street. They came in separately, doing their last minute Christmas shopping. Each loaded down with packages from other stores, Frank (Robert De Niro) and Molly (Meryl Streep) wandered through the store, looking for the perfect gift for their significant others, and then collided on the way out, never dreaming that this collision was just the first time their paths would cross. In *Falling in Love*, Frank and Molly were destined to meet again and again.

Continue west on 57th until you are across from 140 West 57th.

23. 140 West 57th Street. On this spot, the site of the former theme restaurant Planet Hollywood, crazed killers Oleg (Oleg Taktarov) and Emil (Karel Roden) sat at a table and watched on a large TV screen as the home video of their torture and execution of detective Eddie Flemming (Robert De Niro) was broadcast over the airwaves on a tabloid news show, giving them their *15 Minutes* of fame. But pride got the better of them and within minutes, they were fighting over creative credit for the episode. A few minutes later, arson investigator Jordy Warsaw (Ed Burns) came in to make an arrest.

Continue west on 57th until you are across from Carnegie Hall, before reaching Seventh Avenue.

24. Carnegie Hall. 154 West 57th Street. After

developing a crush on world-renowned pianist Henry Orient (Peter Sellers), wide-eyed schoolgirls Valerie Boyd (Tippy Walker) and Marion Gilbert (Merrie Spaeth) came here to attend a concert at which Henry was performing, in *The World of Henry Orient*. But Henry, who had previously noticed the two girls on a number of occasions, and never with good results, was clearly unnerved by their appearance.

They were a long way from their school in East Harlem, but thanks to a tremendous amount of hard work and enthusiasm and some helping hands along the way, particularly from Roberta (Meryl Streep) who had taught them to play the violin, the students had their big-time debut here, in *Music of the Heart*. They played before a packed house, and shared the stage with such music world luminaries as Isaac Stern and Itzhak Perlman.

Continue west on 57th Street, turn right on Seventh Avenue and head north until you reach 59th Street (Central Park South). Turn right on Central Park South and stop in front of the New York Athletic Club.

25. New York Athletic Club. 180 Central Park South. Abruptly leaving this club, Phillip (Cary Grant) stood under the awning to stay out of the rain and asked a friend to arrange for a job for Cathy (Doris Day). Later on, in *That Touch of Mink*, Phillip came charging out of the club in nothing but a towel to hail a cab.

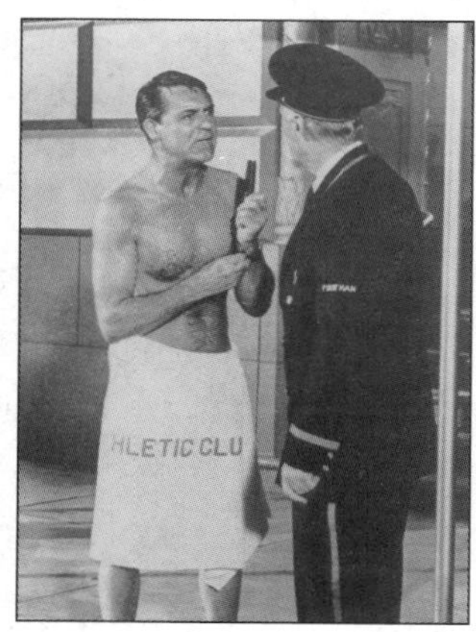

Cross Central Park South to the north side of the street, then glance to your right, in the direction of Sixth Avenue.

26. Central Park South (Between Seventh and Sixth Avenues). Chivalry wasn't dead. At least not where Leopold, Duke of Albany (Hugh Jackman), came from. Or more accurately, *when* Leopold came from. Having passed through a time tunnel of sorts, Leopold found himself defending the honor of the thoroughly modern Kate McKay (Meg Ryan) on more than one occasion. And in one particular instance, after a mugger snatched Kate's purse and climbed the low wall into the park, Leopold commandeered a horse from one of the horse-drawn carriages and, with the damsel Kate riding behind him, gave chase through the park, in *Kate and Leopold*.

Turn west on Central Park South (the park should be on your right) and head west toward Columbus Circle. Stop across from the large building at 240 Central Park South.

27. 240 Central Park South. Plucked from the obscurity of a small town, he grew to be a fixture on radio, then television. But he made some bad choices along the way and his fall was as rapid as his rise. And at the end of *A Face in the Crowd*, "Lonesome" Rhodes (Andy Griffith) screamed from a room near the top of this building, while Marsha (Patricia Neal) and Mel (Walter Matthau) stood on the street in front,

realizing that Rhodes had reached the end of his meteoric ascent and would soon be, once again, just another face in the crowd.

Continue heading west until you reach Columbus Circle. Turn to the right and stop before the large monument at the entrance to Central Park, a memorial to the "valiant seamen who perished on the Maine."

28. Columbus Circle. Memorial to Seamen of the Maine. A priest should not be having such thoughts, but young Brian Flynn (Edward Norton) couldn't help himself. Realizing that he was in love with his childhood friend Anna (Jenna Elfman), a forlorn and lovelorn Father Brian sat on the base of this statue and bemoaned his unenviable dilemma, in *Keeping the Faith*.

You have now reached the end of **Walking Tour 1: The Plaza and its Neighbors**.

Café des Artistes

Walking Tour 2

THE LINCOLN CENTER LOOP

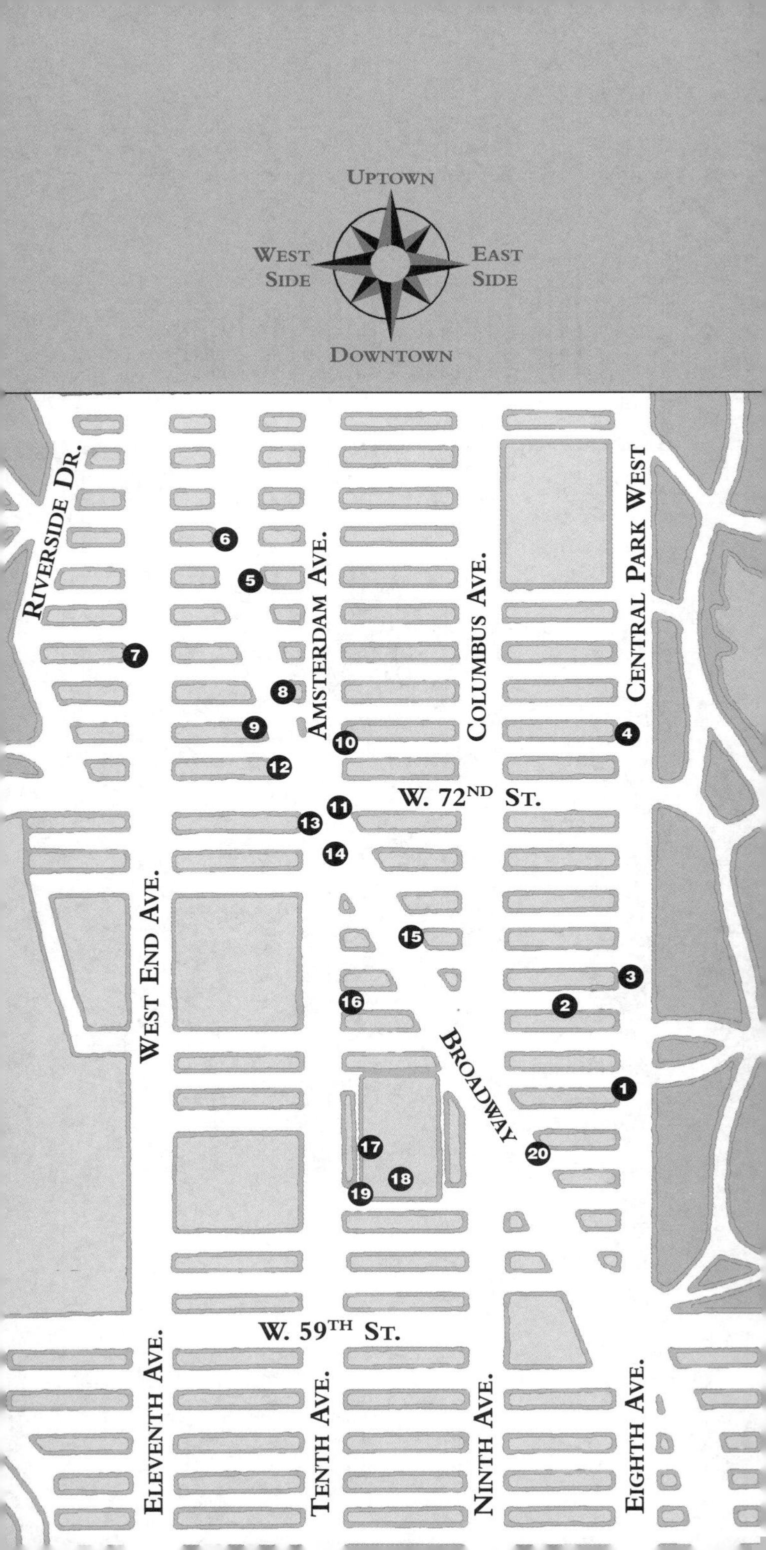

UPTOWN
WEST SIDE
EAST SIDE
DOWNTOWN

RIVERSIDE DR.
AMSTERDAM AVE.
COLUMBUS AVE.
CENTRAL PARK WEST
W. 72ND ST.
WEST END AVE.
BROADWAY
W. 59TH ST.
ELEVENTH AVE.
TENTH AVE.
NINTH AVE.
EIGHTH AVE.
1
2
3
4
5
6
7
8
9
10
11
12
13
14
15
16
17
18
19
20

Walking Tour 2

The Lincoln Center Loop

Once the turf of the Jets and the Sharks, whose battleground in *West Side Story* was razed by the construction of Lincoln Center for the Performing Arts in the 60s, this area of Manhattan has become one of the most artistically and culturally rich in the world.

Serviced by a multitude of trains and buses, Columbus Circle is a natural hub and a great place to start **Walking Tour 2**. If you have just completed **Walking Tour 1**, you need walk north only a few short blocks on Central Park West to get to the first Location of this Tour. If not, then follow the suggested routes below.

If you choose to get to the starting point by public transportation, you may use any of these subway or bus lines (but the following list is by no means exhaustive):

FROM THE NORTH

Subways

- **1** or **2** southbound to 66th Street. Walk east on 66th to Central Park West, then south to 65th Street.
- **B** or **C** southbound to 72nd Street. Walk south on Central Park West to 65th Street.

Buses

- **M5** southbound on Riverside Drive, then Broadway, to 65th Street. Walk east on 65th to Central Park West.
- **M7** southbound on Columbus Avenue to

65th Street. Walk east on 65th to Central Park West.

- **M10** southbound on Central Park West to 65th Street.
- **M104** southbound on Broadway to 65th Street. Walk east on 65th to Central Park West.

FROM THE SOUTH

SUBWAYS

- **1** or **2** northbound to 66th Street. Walk east on 66th to Central Park West, then south to 65th Street.
- **A**, **B**, **C** or **D** northbound to Columbus Circle. Walk north on Central Park West to 65th Street.

BUSES

- **M5** or **M7** northbound on Avenue of the Americas to 59th Street, then westbound on 59th, then northbound on Broadway, to 65th Street. Walk east on 65th to Central Park West.
- **M10** northbound on Hudson Street, then Eighth Avenue, then Central Park West, to 65th Street.
- **M104** northbound on Eighth Avenue, then Broadway, to 65th Street. Walk east on 65th to Central Park West.

FROM THE EAST

SUBWAYS

- **7** or **42nd Street Shuttle** to Times Square. Transfer to **1** or **2** northbound to 66th Street. Walk east on 66th to Central Park West, then south to 65th Street.

BUSES

- **M72** westbound on 72nd Street, then southbound on Fifth Avenue, then westbound on 66th Street, to Central Park West and 66th.

FROM THE WEST

BUSES

- **M72** eastbound on 72nd Street, then southbound on Central Park West, to 66th Street. Walk south on Central Park West to 65th Street.

Get to the west side of Central Park West and 65th Street and walk south the short distance until you are in front of The Prasada, at 50 Central Park West.

1. The Prasada. 50 Central Park West. They had a very strange relationship, lawyer Gordon Hocheiser (George Segal) and his senile mother (Ruth Gordon), who was given to asking on a pretty regular basis, *Where's Poppa?* The two of them lived in this building and even at the end of the movie, the bizarre dynamic between them was not quite clear.

The Prasada was also home to Broadway star Sally Ross (Lauren Bacall), who had many fans, but only one (Michael Biehn) who could consider himself *The Fan*. He had a terrible effect on Sally and those around her, and made all of their lives a living hell.

Turn right and walk north on Central Park West until you reach the far corner of 67th Street. Turn left on 67th and walk the short distance until you are in front of 1 West 67th.

2. 1 West 67th Street. The Templetons, Bill (John Beck), Janice (Marsha Mason) and their daughter Ivy (Susan Swift) lived in splendor in a spacious, multi-level apartment in this building. But when Mr. Hoover (a young Anthony Hopkins, looking like a cross between Rowan Atkinson's Mr. Bean and Major Healy from the television show "I Dream of Jeannie") showed up, making the unfathomable claim that their little Ivy was the reincarnation of his daughter, *Audrey Rose*, who had died in a fiery car crash, they thought he was nuts. But they would soon learn that he wasn't.

Return to Central Park West, turn left and walk north until you reach the far side of 68th Street. Turn and notice a sewer plate on Central Park West, a short distance from the curb.

3. Central Park West and 68th Street. Sewer Plate. After the longest night of their lives, having been forced to sleep in Central Park because the hotel gave away their room, small town denizens George (Jack Lemmon) and Gwen (Sandy Dennis), had had enough. They stood on this corner and argued about what to do next. George then walked out into the street and onto a sewer plate, fortuitously stepping aside just before steam from below blew the plate into the sky. For these *Out of Towners*, where everything that could go wrong did, it was the final straw.

Continue north on Central Park West until you get to 135 Central Park West, which is just past 73rd Street.

4. The Langham. 135 Central Park West (between 73rd and 74th Streets). He may

have made a good living, but Jonathan Balser (Richard Benjamin) did very little to make his wife feel appreciated. So much did he take her for granted that Tina (Carrie Snodgrass) decided to take comfort in the arms of another man (Frank Langella). The unhappy Balsers, and their two kids, lived in this building, in *Diary of a Mad Housewife*.

Continue north on Central Park West and turn left on 76th Street. Head west on 76th until you reach Broadway. Turn right on Broadway and head north until you reach Ruby Foo's (between 77th and 78th Streets).

5. Ruby Foo's. 2182 Broadway. His wife was using their newfound wealth to try and fit into High Society, but Ray (Woody Allen) preferred eating pizza and drinking beer. While passing by here one afternoon in *Small Time Crooks*, Ray was greeted by his wife's cousin May (Elaine May), who was dining inside. Although this restaurant offers food much finer than pizza and beer, Ray and May seemed to share more down-to-earth tastes than Ray and his wife.

Before heading south, turn back and look one block up Broadway, at the large building on the west side of Broadway, between 78th and 79th Streets.

6. The Apthorp. 2211 Broadway (between 78th and 79th Streets). This is where Vera Cicero (Diane Lane) lived and consorted with the likes of Dutch Schultz (James Remar) and Dixie Dwyer (Richard Gere), in *The Cotton Club*.

Turn back and head south on Broadway. At 75th Street, cross Broadway and head west until you reach West End Avenue. 325 should be directly across West End Avenue from you.

7. 325 West End Avenue. They thought it would be a step in the right direction when they moved out of this building and headed for the suburbs. But the Everhearts (Katherine Ross and Peter Masterson), along with their daughter (a 7-year-old Mary Stuart Masterson) didn't quite know what they were getting themselves into, when they put down roots in the seemingly idyllic town of Stepford, Connecticut. But they would soon learn why the town was just a little bit too peaceful, in *The Stepford Wives*.

Return to Broadway and turn right, heading south until you are across from the Beacon Theater, just north of 74th Street.

8. Beacon Theater. 2124 Broadway. After blowing up an underground garage, the so-called Party Crasher (Stephen Lang) ran in here, followed closely by Lieutenant John Moss (James Woods), for what should have been the final showdown. But nothing ever seemed to work easily for Moss, and ever since movie star Nick Lang (Michael J. Fox) started tagging along, everything was done *The Hard Way*.

Continue south on Broadway to 74th Street. The Ansonia is across 74th Street from you.

9. The Ansonia. 2109 Broadway (at 74th Street). There was a time when Willie Clark (Walter Matthau) had been one half of the legendary vaudeville team of Lewis and Clark with long-time partner and current nemesis, Al Lewis (George Burns), otherwise known as *The Sunshine Boys*. But many years had passed since then, and Willie spent his days living a curmudgeonly existence in a cluttered apartment in this building, where his primary contact with the outside world was the weekly visit from his nephew Ben (Richard Benjamin).

This same building was home to esteemed psychiatrist Dr. Nathan Conrad (Michael Douglas), his wife Aggie (Famke Janssen) and their daughter Jessie (Skye McCole Bartusiak), in *Don't Say a Word*. They went to sleep on the night before Thanksgiving, hoping to see the Bart Simpson balloon in the next day's parade, but when Dr. Conrad woke to find that young Jessie had been kidnapped as a way to force him to work his magic on a troubled teen, the whole idea of Thanksgiving took on a new meaning for all of them.

Continue south on the west side of Broadway until you are halfway between 72nd and 73rd Streets. Turn left and notice the bar on the corner of 73rd Street and Amsterdam Avenue.

10. P & G Bar/Café. 279 Amsterdam Avenue (at 73rd Street). Although his girlfriend wanted him to follow a more secure and more legitimate career path, Gary (Andy Garcia) thought he had *Just the Ticket* to a great life, and his habits were hard to break. After long days of scalping tickets to various sporting and cultural events around town, Gary and his friends came here to eat, drink and unwind.

Tour 2

Continue south until you reach 72nd Street. Look east toward Gray's Papaya.

11. Gray's Papaya. 2090 Broadway (at 72nd Street). He finally got Sontee (Regina King) to go on a date with him, and he took her here. But Lance Barton (Chris Rock) had great difficulty realizing that Sontee and everyone else didn't see him as the *Down to Earth* person he used to be, but as Charles Wellington, the middle-aged white man whose body he had been given to use on a temporary basis. And when, trying to impress Sontee, he started singing rap, he got his lights punched out by some bystanders.

Turn around and notice the large building towering overhead, on the northwest corner of Broadway and 72nd Street.

12. The Alexandria. 201 West 72nd Street (at Broadway). Her face graced the pages of fashion magazines, but her personal life was in complete disarray. Her best prospect seemed to be a self-absorbed actor named Bob (Maxwell Caulfield), who only called when he was feeling low. Her name was Sahara (Bridgette Wilson), she lived in this building, and she didn't reveal until the end of the movie that she wasn't a real blonde, in *The Real Blonde*.

Turn and head south on Broadway until you reach 71st Street. Then turn and look back at the rear entrance to the 72nd Street Subway Station, in the middle of Broadway.

13. 72nd Street Subway Station. South Entrance. A rally in the Bronx got out of hand and after a shooting, utter chaos ensued. The street gang known as *The Warriors* knew they had a long night ahead of them in trying to return to their home turf, in Coney Island, Brooklyn, a long distance away. They hopped the subway, but when that didn't work out as planned, a few of them got off here and raced through this doorway, only to find a rival gang, with painted faces, wearing baseball uniforms and waving baseball bats. The Warriors fled and the bat wielders followed in hot pursuit.

Now look around where you are standing, at the various corners abutting Broadway and 71st Street, including the benches on the median between the uptown and downtown lanes on Broadway. Welcome to Needle Park.

14. Needle Park. Broadway and 71st Street to 72nd Street. The neighborhood has changed significantly, and most of the stores and eateries from those days have evolved into what you see, but back in the early 70s Bobby (Al Pacino), Helen (Kitty Winn) and the rest of their so-called friends spent a good deal of time hanging around this area, scoring drugs or using drugs. It was *The Panic in Needle Park*, and they would learn that good times are often followed by bad, and a friend was only a friend until somebody else came along and made him a better offer.

Continue south on Broadway until you are across from 2000 Broadway (just north of 69th Street).

15. 2000 Broadway (at 69th Street). Before he was given a "glimpse" of what might have been, finance wiz Jack Campbell (Nicolas Cage) lived in the largest apartment in this building and seemed to have no regrets about the path his life had taken. But after waking in "his" bed in a suburban home with his wife Kate (Tea Leoni) and their kids, Jack figured he was just having a bad dream. He drove into Manhattan and came here, only to learn that nobody had any idea who he was. He had ceased to be The Business Man, and had become, instead, *The Family Man.*

Continue south on Broadway and turn right on 67th Street. Walk west on 67th until you reach 145 West 67th Street.

Tour 2

16. Tower 67. 145 West 67th Street. In the rain, Assistant District Attorney Al Reilly (Timothy Hutton) pulled up to this building's entrance and pleaded with his ex-girlfriend, Nancy (Jenny Lumet) to let him talk to her. Nancy was now dating a shady character involved in a case Al was prosecuting and Nancy didn't want to talk. When she started to walk away, Al backed his car onto the sidewalk, blocking her path. Her means of escape cut off, Nancy finally got into the car, in *Q & A*.

Return to Broadway, turn right and head south until you reach Lincoln Center. Veer onto Columbus Avenue and walk along the plaza until you reach the fountain in the center of the plaza. Face the Metropolitan Opera House, sitting grandly on the far side of the fountain.

17. Lincoln Center for the Performing Arts. Metropolitan Opera House. 30 Lincoln Center Plaza. To keep peace in the family, Alby

Sherman (Elliott Gould) ended things with his non-Jewish girlfriend and agreed to date Cheryl (Carol Kane), of whom his family approved. On one of their dates, Cheryl and Alby came here to see an opera. Although Cheryl enjoyed the performance, Alby slept through most of it, in *Over the Brooklyn Bridge*.

Turn left and face The New York State Theater.

18. New York State Theater. 20 Lincoln Center Plaza. In *Fame*, some wanted to dance, some wanted to sing, some wanted to act and some wanted to play musical instruments. But in *Center Stage*, students wanted to do one thing, and that was to dance. Much of the action in the film was set in this building and around the plaza itself.

Walk to the far side of the fountain and head left, between the New York State Theater and the Metropolitan Opera House. You should soon be in Damrosch Park, a small concrete oasis, with a large bandshell stage at the far end.

19. Damrosch Park. Lincoln Center. During a frenetic day, the seemingly ordinary people who became disciples in *Godspell* sang and danced their way throughout New York City. In one scene, they related the story of Lazarus while here in this park, and even put on a show on stage, although nobody else was around to enjoy it.

Re-trace your steps back to the fountain, then turn right and leave Lincoln Center. Descend the steps to Columbus Avenue and turn right. Walk one block to 63rd Street, turn left and head east until you are in front of Fiorello's.

20. Fiorello's. 1900 Broadway. While Broadway director Joe Gideon (Roy Scheider) was laid up in the hospital, recovering from a heart attack, the producers and backers of his show were more interested in the bottom line. Not certain of when or if Gideon would return to work, they met here with another director, Lucas Sergeant (John Lithgow), in *All That Jazz*, and threw out to him the possibility of his stepping in and taking over the reins from Joe Gideon.

Walking Tour 2: The Lincoln Center Loop ends at this point.

POMANDER
WALK

Walking Tour 3

Columbia to Columbus

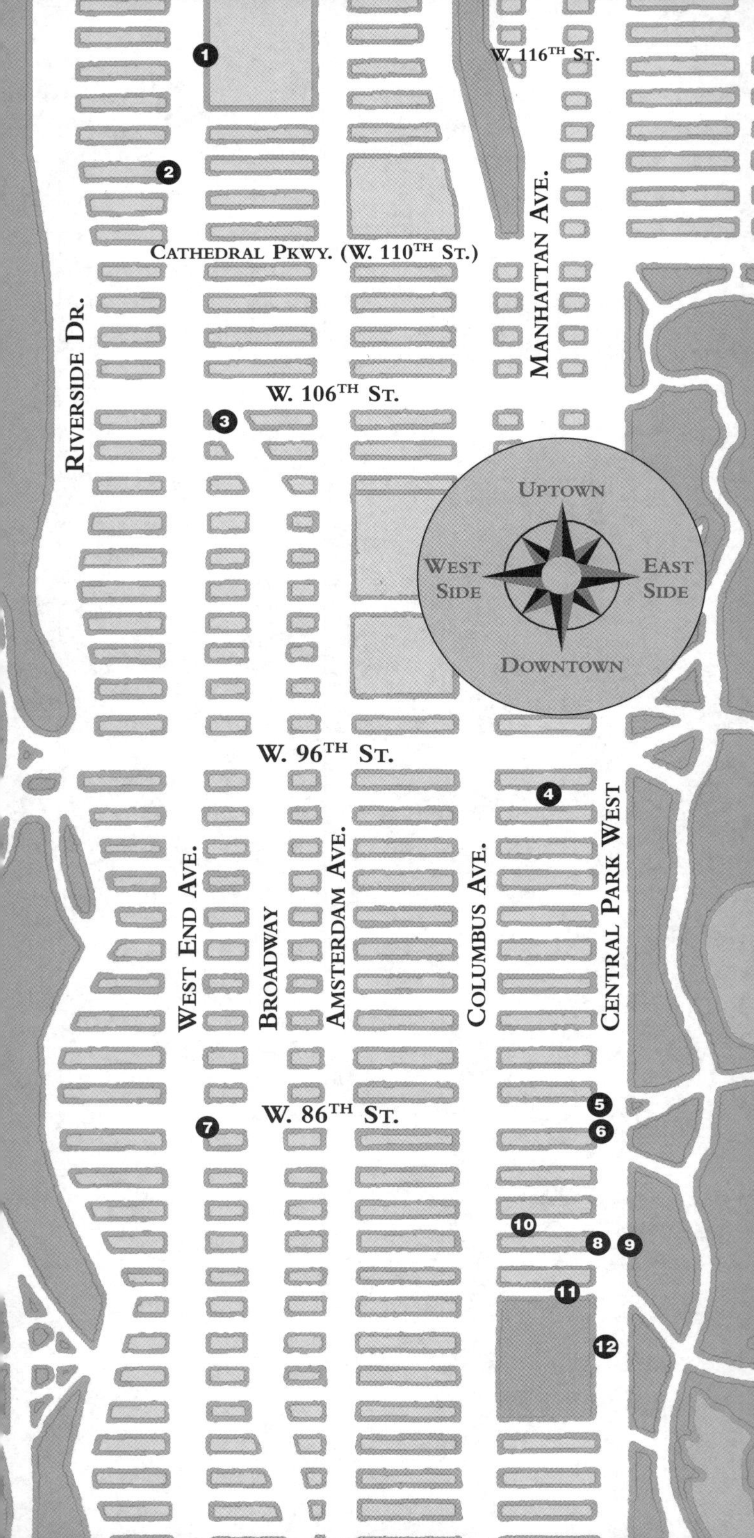
W. 116TH ST.
CATHEDRAL PKWY. (W. 110TH ST.)
MANHATTAN AVE.
RIVERSIDE DR.
W. 106TH ST.
UPTOWN
WEST SIDE
EAST SIDE
DOWNTOWN
W. 96TH ST.
WEST END AVE.
BROADWAY
AMSTERDAM AVE.
COLUMBUS AVE.
CENTRAL PARK WEST
W. 86TH ST.
1
2
3
4
5
6
7
8
9
10
11
12

Walking Tour 3

Columbia To Columbus

Put your walking shoes on because **Walking Tour 3: Columbia to Columbus** covers a lot of ground, but the locations to be seen will make it well worth the trip.

Walking Tour 3: Columbia to Columbus begins at 116th Street and Broadway, in front of the entrance to Columbia University. If you choose to get to the starting point by public transportation, you may use any of the following subway or bus lines (although the following list is by no means exhaustive):

FROM THE NORTH

SUBWAYS

- **1** southbound to 116th Street.

BUSES

- **M4** or **M104** southbound on Broadway to 116th Street.
- **M5** southbound on Broadway, then Riverside Drive, to 116th Street. Walk east on 116th to Broadway.

FROM THE SOUTH

SUBWAYS

- **1** northbound to 116th Street.

BUSES

- **M5** northbound on Broadway, then Riverside Drive, to 116th Street. Walk east on 116th to Broadway.
- **M104** northbound to 116th Street.

FROM THE EAST

Buses

- **M4** northbound on Madison Avenue, then westbound on 110th Street, then northbound on Broadway, to 116th Street.
- **M66, M72, M79, M86** or **M96** westbound to Broadway. Transfer to **M104** northbound on Broadway, to 116th Street.

Your starting point is Broadway and 116th Street. The gates to Columbia University should loom before you. Feel free to go through the gates and admire the campus from within.

Tour 3

1. **Columbia University. 116th Street and Broadway**. Paul (David Selby) was a history professor here and one day, in *Up the Sandbox*, his wife Margaret (Barbra Streisand) stopped by after her doctor's appointment to tell him that she was pregnant, but he was in a meeting, and she didn't get the chance. The academic life must have made an impression on Ms. Streisand, though, because years later, she, too, would play a professor at this school, in *The Mirror Has Two Faces* (see *Manhattan on Film*, **Walking Tour 3**, Location 1).

If you entered the grounds of Columbia, return to Broadway and turn left. If not, turn right and head south on Broadway until you reach 112th Street. If you are on the west side of the street, turn around and note the store on the corner with the flowers out front. If you are on the east side of the street, note the same store across Broadway.

2. **Broadway and 112th Street. Northwest corner**. After a reward had been offered for his capture, Nicky (Adam Sandler), Satan's childlike son, stopped at this shop to smell the flowers out front. But people recognized him and pretty soon, a large crowd was chasing *Little Nicky* down Broadway. For the record, in case you didn't rec-

ognize it on your own, the restaurant on the northeast corner of this intersection (Tom's) was the façade of the Coffee Shop that was frequented by Jerry, Elaine, George and Kramer, on "Seinfeld."

Continue walking south on Broadway. At 107th Street, Broadway veers left and West End Avenue begins. Bear left and stay on Broadway, continuing south, until you reach Smoke, at 2751 Broadway.

3. Smoke. 2751 Broadway (between 105th and 106th Streets). After a tough day on the job, three good cops named Artie (Michael Keaton), Stevie (Anthony LaPaglia) and Felix (Benjamin Bratt) thought about going for a drink at the bar that was located here, but when they saw their commanding officer Lt. Danny Quinn (Kevin Conway) inside, they decided to pick a different place to spend their down time, in *One Good Cop.*

Continue south until you reach 95th Street. Turn left on 95th and head east until you are in front of 12 West 95th Street (between Columbus Avenue and Central Park West).

4. 12 West 95th Street. She had lived here for years, but after her husband died, Kay (Sally Field) had been unable to face the memories. But as the day for her wedding to Rupert (Jeff Bridges) approached, Kay realized it was better to face her demons than to ignore them. Despite the misgivings of everyone around her, Kay

started to move back in. But that proved more difficult than she had imagined, especially when the ghost of her husband, Jolly (James Caan), kept making an appearance. But with the help of Jolly, whose many visits served a purpose, Kay was able to bid him a final goodbye, in *Kiss Me Goodbye.*

Continue east on 95th Street, turn right on Central Park West and head south until you reach 87th Street. Slow down until you are in front of 262 Central Park West.

5. 262 Central Park West (between 86th and 87th Streets). Marjorie (Natalie Wood) was still in school and still lived here with her parents, but a summer with Noel Airman (Gene Kelly) was going to make her grow up fast. And although she wanted a life in the theater, she would eventually question whether Noel was going to figure in her plans, in *Marjorie Morningstar.*

Continue south to the corner of 86th Street.

6. 86th Street and Central Park West. In a car chase that is still one of the most memorable in screen history, New York City cop Buddy (Roy Scheider) pursued one of the bad guys through just about every inch of Manhattan's streets. At one point, the two cars raced up Central Park West and made screeching left turns onto 86th Street and continued on their way, heading west toward the Hudson River, in *The Seven-Ups.*

You now have the option of taking a short detour. In the spirit of full disclosure, I will tell you that it is for one location and will add roughly 20 minutes to the duration of the walking tour, but for fans of Michael Douglas, Kathleen Turner and the adventure classic *Romancing the Stone*, it is well worth the trip. If you choose to defer Location 7 until another time, skip ahead to the directions to Location 8.

If you loved *Romancing the Stone* and are game for this little detour, turn right on 86th Street and walk west (away from Central Park) until you reach West End Avenue (four blocks away). Turn left on West End Avenue and stop at the building on the southeast corner of West End and 86th Street.

7. 530 West End Avenue (at 86th Street). Joan Wilder (Kathleen Turner) wrote novels about romance and adventure. Her heroines were beautiful, her heroes dashing and brave. And then, on a trip to Colombia, her life imitated her art and she had the adventure of a lifetime, in *Romancing the Stone*. After she returned to New York, Joan handed in a novel that made her agent weep, and resumed her normal, staid life. But not for long. Returning home with groceries, she was astounded to find her dashing real-life hero Jack Colton (Michael Douglas) polishing his boat in front of this building. She discarded the groceries, admired Jack's boots—which resembled a certain reptile they had battled in Colombia—and climbed aboard to head off on another adventure.

If you took the *Romancing the Stone* detour, head south on West End Avenue and turn left on 83rd Street. Walk east on 83rd until you reach Central Park West, then turn right. If you did not take the detour, continue heading south on Central Park West until you reach 83rd Street. In either case, head south on Central Park West until you reach number 225, which is halfway between 82nd and 83rd Streets.

8. 225 Central Park West (between 82nd and 83rd Streets). After dumping the only girl he ever loved, Sebastian (Ryan Phillippe) camped out across the street from this building, where Annette (Reese Witherspoon) lived, and waited for her to read his journal. He hoped she would realize that he truly loved her, and that his *Cruel Intentions* were a thing of the past.

Look toward Central Park. You may see big shots from the world of television news.

9. Along the Central Park Wall. They were both powerful people in the world of television news programming, and for a while, they did more than just work for the same *Network*: they shared a romance torrid enough that it caused Max (William Holden) to leave his wife for Diane (Faye Dunaway). Trying to get away from the rigors of their industry, they took a stroll and stopped here to share a few affectionate moments.

Tour 3

Head back north on Central Park West and turn left on 83rd Street. Walk west until you are in front of 46 West 83rd Street.

10. 46 West 83rd Street. There were 8 million stories in *The Naked City*, and one of them took place here. Although the building's address was shown to be number 52 in the movie, this is where a woman's body was found, a crime the police did their best to solve before the final credits started to roll.

Continue west on 83rd Street. Turn left on Columbus Avenue and walk two blocks south to 81st Street. Turn left on 81st and stop across from the planets suspended inside the glass cube that is the Hayden Planetarium's Rose Center for Earth and Space, just before Central Park West.

11. Hayden Planetarium's Rose Center for Earth and Space. 81st Street, just west of Central Park West. Jamal (Rob Brown) was doing his best to fit in at his new school, and his new friend Claire (Anna Paquin) was doing her best to make his transition easier. Later on, Jamal would devote his energies to *Finding Forrester*, but right now, he just wanted to find a friend. One afternoon they came here, discussed how Claire ended up at the Mailor-Callow School and the possibility that their friendship might move to another level.

Tour 3

Continue east and turn right on Central Park West. Head south until you reach the subway entrance just south of the Museum's entrance (past the statue of Theodore Roosevelt).

12. Subway Entrance. South of Entrance to Museum of Natural History. She lifted his wallet and Mikey (Michael J. Fox) chased her down these stairs to the subway. But when Angie

(Christina Vidal) pulled a small knife on him and kicked him, Mikey knew he was in over his head and let her go. But when he found her pulling the same stunt on someone else outside the museum, he stood and watched her wonderful display of histrionics. Then, in *Life With Mikey*, Mikey did what any talent agent in his shoes would do: He tried to sign her up for representation.

You have now reached the last location on **Walking Tour 3: Columbia to Columbus**.

The Stanhope
NEW YORK

Walking Tour 4

The Miracle Mile

E. 96TH ST.
UPTOWN
WEST SIDE
EAST SIDE
DOWNTOWN
E. 86TH ST.
FIFTH AVE.
MADISON AVE.
PARK AVE.
LEXINGTON AVE.
THIRD AVE.
SECOND AVE.
FIRST AVE.
E. 72ND ST.
E. 59TH ST.
1
2
3
4
5
6
7
8
9
10
11
12
13
14
15
16
17
18
19
20
21

Walking Tour 4

THE MIRACLE MILE

Although there are places throughout the country that have earned the moniker "the miracle mile," for purposes of this book, the miracle mile is an elegant stretch of Manhattan that runs the length of the western three avenues of the Upper East Side (namely, Fifth, Madison and Park Avenues). And the term is every bit as accurate for this stretch of the city as for any other.

Walking Tour 4: The Miracle Mile begins at 64th Street and Madison Avenue. If you choose to get to the starting point by public transportation, you may use any of the following subway or bus lines (although the following list is by no means exhaustive):

FROM THE NORTH

SUBWAYS

- **4 or 5** southbound to 86th Street. Switch to **6** southbound to 68th Street. Walk west on 68th to Madison Avenue, then south on Madison to 64th Street.
- **6** southbound to 68th Street, then follow directions for **4** or **5** southbound.

BUSES

- **M1, M2, M3** or **M4** southbound on Fifth Avenue to 64th Street. Walk east on 64th to Madison Avenue.
- **M101, M102** or **M103** southbound on Lexington Avenue to 64th Street. Walk west on 64th to Madison Avenue.

FROM THE SOUTH

SUBWAYS

- **4, 5** or **6** northbound to 59th Street. Walk north to 64th Street, then west on 64th to Madison Avenue.
- **F** northbound to Lexington Avenue and 63rd Street. Walk west on 63rd to Madison Avenue, then north on Madison to 64th Street.

BUSES

- **M1, M2** or **M3** northbound on Park Avenue South, then Park Avenue, then Madison Avenue, to 64th Street.
- **M4** northbound on Madison Avenue to 64th Street.
- **M101, M102** or **M103** northbound on Third Avenue to 64th Street. Walk west on 64th to Madison Avenue.

FROM THE EAST

BUSES

- **M66** westbound on 67th Street to Madison Avenue. Walk south on Madison to 64th Street.
- **M72** westbound on 72nd Street to Fifth Avenue, then southbound on Fifth to 66th Street. Walk east on 66th to Madison Avenue, then south on Madison to 64th.

FROM THE WEST

BUSES

- **M66** or **M72** eastbound to Madison Avenue and 64th Street.
- **M79, M86** or **M96** eastbound to Fifth Avenue. Transfer to **M1, M2, M3** or **M4** southbound on Fifth, to 64th Street. Walk east on 64th to Madison Avenue.

Assuming you have successfully gotten yourself to Madison Avenue and 64th Street, cross to the northeast corner of the intersection and head east on the north side of 64th until you reach the Plaza Athenee Hotel, at 37 East 64th.

1. Plaza Athenee Hotel. 37 East 64th Street. Re-named the Grand Mark, this hotel is where Mr. Mersault (John Cleese), the fussy hotel concierge made life miserable for *The Out-of-Towners* Henry (Steve Martin) and Nancy (Goldie Hawn) during their stay in New York, and vice versa.

Return to Madison and turn right. Walk north the short distance until you are across Madison from the restaurant La Goulue.

2. La Goulue. 746 Madison Avenue. Her marriage having failed, Judith (Holly Hunter) did her best to get on with her life. She came here for dinner by herself, reading Edith Wharton's "The House of Mirth." Noticing the people around her enjoying themselves, she realized the gaping hole that existed in her life and resolved that it wouldn't be long before she was *Living Out Loud*.

Continue north on the east side of Madison until just south of 66th Street, and stop in front of the store, Krizia.

3. Krizia. 769 Madison Avenue. In the movie *15 Minutes*, this was the location of Ludwig's

Hair Salon, where Daphne (Vera Farmiga), the witness to the first murder committed by the two Eastern European killers, worked. Minutes before Detective Eddie Flemming (Robert De Niro) and arson investigator Jordy Warsaw (Ed Burns) showed up to see what Daphne knew, the killers had paid her a visit and warned her not to talk. Or else.

Cross Madison Avenue and head west on 66th Street until you reach Fifth Avenue. Cross Fifth, turn left and head south until you are halfway between 65th and 66th Streets. The Central Park Zoo is just over the low wall, but don't look there yet.

Tour 4

4. Fifth Avenue, between 65th and 66th Streets. West side of the street. She made a habit of coming to New York on Sundays and on a particular *Sunday in New York*, that is exactly what she did. During her visit, Eileen (Jane Fonda), a wide-eyed innocent from upstate New York, tried to hail a cab from this spot, then boarded a bus headed south. She would soon find herself attached to Mike (Rod Taylor) when her flower got caught on his jacket pocket.

Near the almost identical spot where she boarded the bus as Eileen, Jane Fonda was back a few years later. As Brice Daniels, Fonda was no wide-eyed innocent, but rather a high-priced call girl, and she found herself embroiled in an investigation of the disappearance of one of her occasional clients. In *Klute*, after finally convincing private investigator John Klute (Donald Sutherland) that she had told him everything she could, they met here and Klute gave her the surveillance tapes he had made of her during his investigation. Brice took the tapes and tossed them into a trashcan against the wall.

Now you may approach the wall and peer into the zoo.

5. Central Park Zoo. He was distraught that his wife was off in Reno with some playboy, so he came here to think and get away from the stress of his world. While sitting on a bench, business mogul Timothy Borden (Walter Connolly) struck up a conversation with young Mary Grey (Ginger Rogers), who knew nothing of the finer things in life, which suited Borden just fine. He had had enough of that, and made this *Fifth Avenue Girl* a part of his family's life.

Mary was just what the doctor ordered for Timothy Borden. But when the animals in the zoo needed some attention, they got it from Tommy Donovan (Edward Herrmann), who worked at the zoo. And while Tommy was tending to his animal wards, his brother Michael

Tour 4

(Tim Matheson) was tending to most of the women in Manhattan, in *A Little Sex*. On one occasion, Michael came here to ask for some brotherly advice.

If you have the time or the inclination, this might be a good time to visit the zoo. If you do, pay the small admission charge and eventually work your way over to the polar bears. If you choose not to, then just imagine yourself standing near the polar bear habitat.

6. Central Park Zoo. Polar Bear Habitat. Still trying to get his evil brothers back down to hell, but not sure of the form they had taken on earth, Nicky (Adam Sandler) did his best to coax a polar bear into his magic flask. He failed, meeting his fate at the hands (or jaws) of the polar bear, and was sent back to hell, where he had to start all over again, in *Little Nicky*.

Whether you went into the Central Park Zoo or not, find your way back to Fifth Avenue and head north on Fifth until you reach 68th Street. Turn right on 68th and walk the short distance east until you are in front of 16 East 68th Street.

7. 16 East 68th Street. Money alone didn't make him happy. He liked art and he loved the thrill of the chase. In *The Thomas Crown Affair*, wealthy, billionaire industrialist Thomas Crown (Pierce Brosnan) got his hands on whatever pieces of art he liked, using legitimate or not-so-legitimate means. He lived with his artwork and his wealth in this grand home.

Continue east on 68th Street and stop at the near corner of Park Avenue. Turn left, cross 68th Street and stop in front of the first building on the left.

8. 680 Park Avenue. The Americas Society. He didn't live particularly close by, but Jamal Wallace (Rob Brown) had a skill that the administrators of the Mailor-Callow School hoped to capitalize on: his abilities on the basketball court. But Jamal had another talent that gave him more in common with Pulitzer-Prize-winning author William Forrester (Sean Connery) than with most of the faculty or student body at the school, which was located here, in *Finding Forrester.*

Head north on Park Avenue until you reach 71st Street. Turn left on 71st and walk west. Cross Madison Avenue and continue west until you reach number 22.

Tour 4

9. 22 East 71st Street. IMG. Not as famous as some of the other auction houses, this building was the location of Cromwell's Auctioneers and Appraisers, where Michael (Hugh Grant) worked and had to deal with everything from a meddling boss to a gangster who envisioned himself as the next Michelangelo, in *Mickey Blue Eyes.*

Return to Madison Avenue, turn left and walk north on Madison to the far side of 75th Street. Turn left on 75th and head west until you are in front of 7 East 75th Street.

10. 7 East 75th Street. Familiar to ardent fans of television's "The Nanny," this building was the home of Broadway producer Maxwell Sheffield (Charles O'Shaunessy), his children Maggie (Nicholle Tom), Brighton (Benjamin

Salisbury) and Gracie (Madeline Zima), his nosey butler Niles (Daniel Davis) and of course, his irrepressible nanny, Fran Fine (Fran Drescher).

Continue west to Fifth Avenue, turn right on Fifth and walk north to 79th Street. Turn right on 79th and stop in front of the beautiful building on the corner.

11. 2 East 79th Street. The Ukranian Institute. Not exactly a private residence, but it served as such in *Cruel Intentions*. From within its walls, Kathryn (Sarah Michelle Gellar) and her step-brother Sebastian (Ryan Phillippe), the scourges of Manchester Prep, lived here without parental supervision and, from within, hatched a scheme to destroy the lives and reputations of many innocent people.

Return to Fifth Avenue, turn right and head north until you reach the Stanhope Hotel, halfway between 80th and 81st Streets.

12. 995 Fifth Avenue. Stanhope Hotel. Hot-headed superstar Brandon (Leonardo DiCaprio) had the world at his fingertips, and thought nothing of trashing his room, which he considered a right of *Celebrity*. Undeterred, writer Lee Simon (Kenneth Branagh) showed up at Brandon's hotel room, in this hotel, to discuss his screenplay with the tempestuous star.

Continue north on Fifth Avenue to 82nd Street, across Fifth Avenue from the magnificence of the Metropolitan Museum of Art.

13. Metropolitan Museum of Art. Fifth Avenue and 82nd Street. Joe (Robert Walker) had only a few days leave, so the clock was ticking, but he was lucky enough to meet the lovely and friendly Alice (Judy Garland) almost as soon as he got off the train, when he rescued a piece of her shoe from a wayward escalator.

Afterwards, with his puppy dog look and his just-off-the-farm sincerity, Joe convinced Alice to accompany him on a whirlwind tour of New York. In *The Clock*, they saw it all, including this museum.

Tour 4

The museum is also where Rupert (Jeff Bridges) worked in *Kiss Me Goodbye*. He couldn't compete with Jolly (James Caan), the dead husband of his fiancée Kay (Sally Field) and a memorable Broadway star, but he hoped that he wouldn't have to.

The museum was also a favorite of Thomas Crown (Pierce Brosnan). He spent a good deal of time admiring the artwork, and only slightly less time swiping it off the walls. Near the end of *The Thomas Crown Affair*, Crown did the impossible: he returned a painting to the wall, without anyone seeing—although a great many were watching—without using his hands. The scene where Crown and dozens of look-alikes wearing overcoats and derbies out of a Magritte painting and carrying briefcases hustled throughout the museum's corridors, in an attempt to throw off the closed-circuit monitors, was a work of art in and of itself, and not to be missed.

Turn from the museum and head east on 82nd Street. Stop in front of 2 East 82nd Street.

14. 2 East 82nd Street. Although she was a suspect in the murder of one of his patients, Psychiatrist Dr. Sam Rice (Roy Scheider) could not believe she was capable of any such thing. But as he started getting a little too close to the beautiful Brooke Reynolds (Meryl Streep), Dr. Rice may have lost his ability to figure out whether he could trust her or not. Miss Reynolds, the mysterious suspect, lived here, in *Still of the Night*. And Dr. Rice came by one night to see if his suspicions were correct.

Tour 4

Continue east on 82nd and stop in front of 22 East 82nd Street.

15. 22 East 82nd Street. She found her live-in boyfriend in bed with a model, and decided it was time to make other living arrangements. So Amanda (Monica Potter), who happened to work at the Metropolitan Museum of Art just up the block, answered an ad and ended up moving into this building, where she would soon be *Head Over Heels* for Jim Winston (Freddie Prinze, Jr.), while sharing an apartment with the last "four non-smoking models on the island of Manhattan."

Return to Fifth Avenue, turn right and walk north until you pass 88th Street and reach the Guggenheim Museum.

16. Guggenheim Museum. 1071 Fifth Avenue (between 88th and 89th Streets). Having just learned of their father's death, Ophelia (Julia Stiles) and Laertes (Liev Schreiber) confronted the wicked Claudius (Kyle MacLachlan) near the upper part of the Guggenheim, in *Hamlet.* At one point, Ophelia screamed at the top of her lungs. In the museum, the echo can still be heard.

Continue north on Fifth Avenue and turn right on 91st Street. Stop at the first building in, on the south side of the street.

17. 2 East 91st Street. National Design Museum. Eddy Duchin (Tyrone Power) was used to playing the piano at parties as part of the musical entertainment, so when he was invited to be a guest at a fancy party given by the Wadsworths, who lived here, he not only jumped at the chance, but even bought a second-hand car to get him there. He would go on to marry and have a son, and he would visit this home again and again over the years. In *The Eddy Duchin Story*, the Wadsworths and their home became a very big part of his life.

Eddy Duchin became rich and famous, just like the writer Liz Hamilton (Jacqueline Bisset). In *Rich and Famous*, Liz showed up here for a meeting of the committee whose job it was to select the year's best piece of American fiction.

Look across 91st to the large building on the north side of the street.

18. 1 East 91st Street. His girlfriend Ingrid (Dyan Cannon) lived in the building, which gave him the inside track, so Duke Anderson (Sean Connery) decided to target the entire building for a break-in, for which he served as the mastermind, in *The Anderson Tapes.*

Return to Fifth Avenue, turn right and head north until you reach 1136 Fifth Avenue, which is between 94th and 95th Streets.

19. 1136 Fifth Avenue. Struggling stand-up comic Lance Barton (Chris Rock) showed up at this building and the doorman, mistaking him for a messenger, directed him around to the service entrance. Understandably, Lance took offense at the doorman's put down, but not too much, since he was, in fact, a messenger. But after his body was taken away by the "angels" before its time, Lance was temporarily given the body of Mr. Charles Wellington, who had lived in this same building before his untimely demise, in *Down to Earth*. With the assistance of King (Chazz Palminteri), an otherworldly figure, Lance surveyed his options outside the building.

Tour 4

Return to 94th Street and turn left. Walk east to the east side of Madison Avenue, turn right and walk south on Madison to 93rd Street. Stop in front of The Corner Bookstore.

20. The Corner Bookstore. 1313 Madison Avenue (at 93rd Street). Helene (Anne Bancroft) loved books. Especially old books. And most especially, books by British authors. But frustrated by her inability to find such books in

New York, where she visited this bookstore, among others, in her search for her precious volumes, she finally had to search elsewhere. Luckily, she discovered a well-stocked bookstore located at *84 Charing Cross Road*, London.

Head east on 93rd Street, one block. Turn right on Park Avenue and walk south to the southwest corner of 92nd Street. Stop at the building on the corner, number 1165.

21. 1165 Park Avenue (at 92nd Street). Before his scheme to use his wife's cookie shop as a "front" so they could drill into a neighboring bank, small-timer Ray (Woody Allen) and his wife Frenchy (Tracey Ullman) had a tough time making ends meet. But after the cookie business took off and they become rich beyond their wildest dreams, they moved into an enormous, if gaudily decorated apartment in this building, in *Small Time Crooks*.

We have now come to the end of **Walking Tour 4: The Miracle Mile**.

J. G.
MELON

Walking Tour 5

THE INLAND EXPRESS

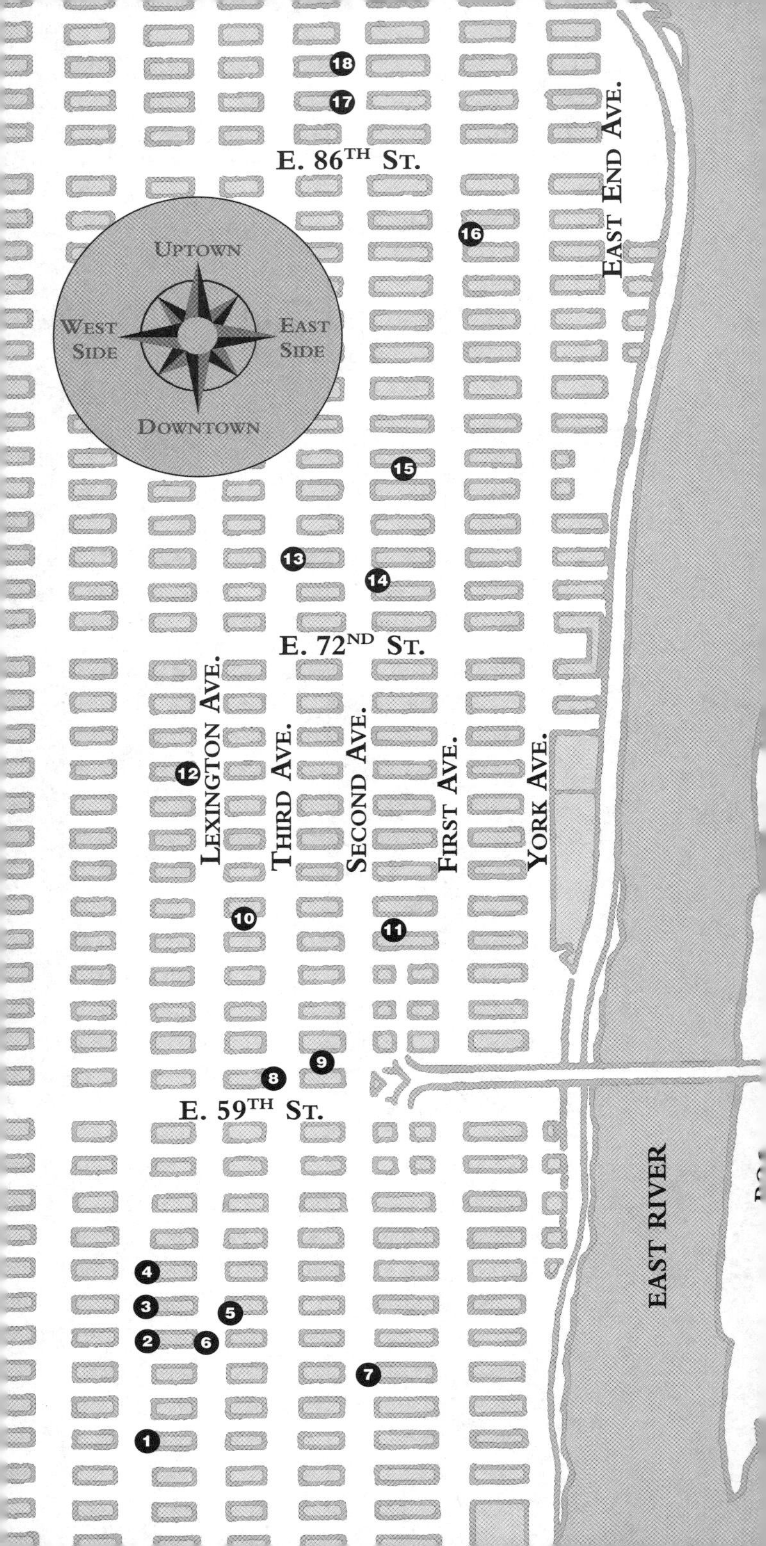

E. 86TH ST.
EAST END AVE.
UPTOWN
WEST SIDE
EAST SIDE
DOWNTOWN
E. 72ND ST.
LEXINGTON AVE.
THIRD AVE.
SECOND AVE.
FIRST AVE.
YORK AVE.
E. 59TH ST.
EAST RIVER
1
2
3
4
5
6
7
8
9
10
11
12
13
14
15
16
17
18

Walking Tour 5

The Inland Express

In Manhattan, many neighborhoods afford wonderful views of the bodies of water that surround this great island. And because it is such a narrow strip of land, no neighborhood is very far from a water view. But the treasures contained in **Walking Tour 5: The Inland Express** owe more to their land-locked nature than to any proximity to New York's rivers.

Walking Tour 5: The Inland Express begins at The Waldorf-Astoria Hotel, one of the most elegant (and most cinematic) of all of New York's accommodations.

If you choose to get to the starting point by public transportation, you may use any of the following subway or bus lines (although the following list is by no means exhaustive):

FROM THE NORTH

Subways

- **4** or **5** southbound to 59th Street. Transfer to **6** southbound to 51st Street. Walk west on 51st, then south on Park Avenue, halfway between 49th and 50th Streets.
- **6** southbound to 51st Street, then follow the directions for the **4** or **5** southbound.

Buses

- **M1**, **M2, M3** or **M4** southbound on Fifth Avenue to 50th Street. Walk east on 50th to Park Avenue.
- **M101, M102** or **M103** southbound on

Lexington Avenue to 50th Street. Walk west on 50th to Park Avenue.

FROM THE SOUTH

SUBWAYS

- **4** or **5** northbound to 42nd Street/Grand Central Station. Transfer to **6** northbound to 51st Street. Walk west on 51st, then south on Park Avenue, halfway between 49th and 50th Streets.
- **6** northbound to 51st Street, then follow the directions for **4** or **5** northbound.
- **E** or **F** northbound, then eastbound, to Lexington Avenue and 53rd Street. Walk west on 53rd, then south on Park, halfway between 49th and 50th Streets.

BUSES

- **M1**, **M2** or **M3** northbound on Park Avenue South, then Madison Avenue, to 50th Street. Walk east on 50th to Park Avenue.
- **M101, M102** or **M103** northbound on Third Avenue to 50th Street. Walk west on 50th to Park Avenue.

FROM THE EAST

BUSES

- **M27** or **M50** westbound on 49th Street to Park Avenue.
- **M31** or **M57** westbound on 57th Street to Lexington Avenue. Transfer to **M101**, **M102** or **M103** southbound on Lexington to 50th Street. Walk west on 50th to Park.

FROM THE WEST

SUBWAYS

- **E** eastbound, to Lexington Avenue and 53rd Street. Walk west on 53rd, then south on Park, halfway between 49th and 50th Streets.

Buses

- **M27** or **M50** eastbound on 50th Street to Park Avenue.
- **M31** or **M57** eastbound on 57th Street to Lexington Avenue. Transfer to **M101**, **M102** or **M103** southbound on Lexington to 50th Street. Walk west on 50th to Park.

However you get to the starting point, **Walking Tour 5: The Inland Express** begins at the Waldorf-Astoria, a hotel known for its excellence and elegance, as well as for its famed lobby statues and fine restaurants. It is constantly playing host to presidents and other visiting dignitaries from all over the world.

1. **The Waldorf-Astoria. 301 Park Avenue (between 49th and 50th Streets).** The majestic Waldorf-Astoria comes in a close second to the Plaza Hotel (see **Walking Tour 1**, Location 1) for its appearances in movies over the years. In fact, the Waldorf has probably played host to a greater variety of film characters over a longer period of time than any other hotel in the world. The Waldorf is where Hazel Flagg (Carole Lombard) was brought for one last fling, before she supposedly succumbed to her life-threatening illness. She got her whirlwind New York adventure, but the news-hungry public who followed her poignant story never got to see her suffering, because her illness was not as dire as everyone was led to believe, proving that, indeed, there is *Nothing Sacred*.

The Waldorf is also where syndicated columnist Randy Morton (Robert Benchley) lived, in *Week-end at the Waldorf*. Morton, who wrote a column entitled "Randy Morton's New York," narrated the story that began with the arrival of a young honeymoon couple, who found that no room was available for them. Taking pity on them, a hotel resident who was going to his country house for the weekend permitted the hotel to give them his room. And that's when the trouble started. And the adventure began.

This hotel is also where Avery Bullard (an unbilled Raoul Freeman), the head of Treadway Furniture Corporation, had stayed during his final business trip to New York which, in *Executive Suite*, proved to be his final trip anywhere.

George (Jack Lemmon) and Gwen (Sandy Dennis) Kellerman encountered a fate like that of the honeymooning couple in *Week-end at the Waldorf*, when they arrived and discovered the hotel had no room for them. But unlike the honeymooners, the Kellermans didn't find a kindly benefactor to give them his room. Instead, these *Out of Towners*, who were here for George's interview, got mugged, rode along during a police chase and spent an awful night in Central Park.

They were good friends and each was *Rich and Famous*, but while Liz (Jacqueline Bisset) stayed at the Algonquin Hotel (see **Walking Tour 9,** Location 25) on trips to New York, Merry Noel Blake (Candice Bergen) opted to stay here.

Most recently, the Waldorf figured prominently in a tale about romance and fate. Jonathan (John Cusack) was glove shopping and bumped into Sara Thomas (Kate Beckinsale) at Bloomingdale's (see Location 8 of this Walking Tour). By the end of the evening, both were convinced there could be something great between them, but Sara wanted to leave things up to destiny, to fate. They came to this hotel—Jonathan thinking his fortunes had suddenly taken a huge leap and that they were going to get a room—but Sara had other ideas. Standing in the deserted lobby, they boarded separate elevators and each had to select a floor. If they selected the same floor, Sara would see it as a sign that they were meant to be together. When Sara reached the twenty-third floor, she waited as long as she could, saw Jonathan's failure to appear as a bad sign and left moments before his elevator arrived at the floor.

It would be years before they would find out whether to believe the signs or not. Later on in *Serendipity*, a dinner celebrating Jonathan's impending wedding to another woman was held in one of the hotel's restaurants.

Continue north on Park Avenue and stop in front of 375 Park Avenue, between 52nd and 53rd Streets.

2. 375 Park Avenue (between 52nd and 53rd Streets). During the filming of a movie within a movie, actress Nicole Oliver (Melanie Griffith), a *Celebrity*, ran from a car parked at the curb, up these plaza steps, and looked up at the word "Help" being spelled out by a skywriting plane, while the rest of the cast, crew and writer Lee Simon (Kenneth Branagh, essentially playing Woody Allen with straighter hair) looked on. The scene was repeated when the story written by Lee, was being made into a movie, at the end of the movie. Or something like that.

Continue north on Park Avenue one block, until you are in front of 399 Park Avenue.

3. 399 Park Avenue (between 53rd and 54th Streets). After the bank officer had been hypnotized, John Dortmunder (Robert Redford) had only to utter the phrase "Afghanistan Bananistan" to get the man to show him to the safe deposit box that held *The Hot Rock*. After taking possession of the priceless jewel, Dortmunder left the bank, which was located here, and got into a waiting car, where he celebrated the success of the caper with his jubilant colleagues.

Continue north on Park until you reach the Susie Cafe, 407 Park Avenue, between 54th and 55th Streets.

4. Susie Cafe. 407 Park Avenue (between 54th and 55th Streets). Alone on Christmas Eve, Jack (Nicolas Cage) went into this deli to buy eggnog, which was the extent of his planned holiday celebration. Inside the store, he diffused a tense situation involving a lottery ticket and wound up being given a special gift by the lottery ticket holder, Cash (Don Cheadle). The gift, as Cash explained to Jack outside the deli, was a "glimpse" of what Jack's life would have been, had he taken a more familial role a number of years ago and traded in his high-powered finance job for a wife and two kids in the suburbs, in *The Family Man*.

Turn around and head south on Park. Turn left on 53rd and head east one block to Lexington Avenue. From the northwest corner of Lexington and 53rd, look diagonally across the street, to the southeast corner.

5. 599 Lexington Avenue (at southeast corner of 53rd Street). The offices of Moramax, the corporation run by Sadie (Bette Midler) and Rose (Lily Tomlin) as unbelievably mismatched "twins" in *Big Business*, were located in this building.

From where you stand, you may either strain your eyes to see it, or walk one block south, to the northwest corner of Lexington Avenue and 52nd Street. Look for a breezy subway grating on the ground at your feet.

6. Lexington Avenue and 52nd Street (Northwest Corner). Subway Grating. Legend has it that they had to re-shoot the scene in Hollywood, because the original filming caused too great a commotion, but it was on this corner that a woman known as The Girl (Marilyn Monroe) stood on a subway grating in a sexy white

skirt and a gust of air from beneath the grating did the rest, creating an image that has achieved cinematic immortality, in *The Seven Year Itch*.

Cross Lexington and head east on 52nd Street until you reach Second Avenue. Look for Clancy's, on the east side of Second, between 51st and 52nd Streets.

7. Clancy's. 978 Second Avenue (between 51st and 52nd Streets). Still trying to figure him out, Amanda (Monica Potter) went to dinner with mystery man Jim (Freddie Prinze, Jr.). But because she was already *Head Over Heels* for him, Amanda's judgment was suspect to her model/roommates who decided to keep an eye on things from a safe corner of the establishment.

Head north on Second Avenue until you reach the north side of 59th Street. Turn left on 59th and stop at Third Avenue. Look across Third, at Bloomingdale's.

8. Bloomingdale's. 1000 Third Avenue. It was the night before Christmas and both Jonathan (John Cusack) and Sara (Kate Beckinsale) had left some shopping to the last minute. They found themselves vying for the same pair of gloves at a counter in this store, but had no idea how that chance encounter would soon have them thinking about things other than Christmas: things like fate, chance, destiny and *Serendipity*.

Walk north on Third one block, to the north side of 60th Street. Turn right on 60th and walk east until you reach Serendipity 3, at 225 East 60th Street.

9. Serendipity 3. 225 East 60th Street. The name means fortunate accident, fate, destiny, providence, kismet. This place also serves some amazing desserts. After their chance encounter in Bloomingdale's, Jonathan and Sara came here, where they shared those desserts. And even though together they enjoyed the best evening of their respective lives, Sara wasn't convinced and she decided to leave their next encounter to fate. Jonathan would have preferred to make more definite plans, but he was smitten with Sara, and in *Serendipity*, he had no choice but to go along with her plan, however risky it appeared to be. Smitten guys will do that.

Turn back on 60th Street and walk west until you reach Lexington Avenue. Turn right and walk north until you reach the far corner of Lexington and 64th. Head east on 64th and stop in front of 165 East 64th Street.

10. 165 East 64th Street. She was young, beautiful, and more than a little naïve. And much to her dismay, she became involved with a conniving, smooth-talking married man, who did what he could to convince her to let him pay for her apartment here, as long as he could stay each Wednesday, while his wife thought he was traveling. It was the perfect arrangement, until Ellen Gordon (Jane Fonda) realized that she was missing out on something that she really wanted and eventually, she had to choose between the married man, John Cleves (Jason Robards), and an available suitor, Cass (Dean Jones), in *Any Wednesday*.

Continue east on 64th Street until just past Third Avenue. Stop across from the hospital entrance at 210 East 64th Street.

11. Manhattan Eye, Ear and Throat Hospital. 210 East 64th Street. Having read about a surgeon who was performing some amazing surgeries to cure blindness, advertising world hotshot Amy (Mira Sorvino) brought sight-challenged masseuse Virgil (Val Kilmer) here for experimental eye surgery. Thanks to a talented team of doctors, Virgil was able to see, although Amy turned out to be the one with blinders on, in *At First Sight*.

Tour 5

Return to Third Avenue, turn right, and head north to 68th Street. Turn left on 68th and walk west until you reach Lexington Avenue. Note the large façade of Hunter College on the west side of the street.

12. Hunter College of the City of New York. 68th Street and Lexington Avenue. Marjorie Morganstern (Natalie Wood) attended this college and had an interest in the theater. But it wasn't until she signed on with well-

known director Noel Airman (Gene Kelly), both onstage and off, that Marjorie learned a good deal more about acting, a great deal more about herself, and acquired a new stage name to boot, in *Marjorie Morningstar.*

Turn right on Lexington and head north until you reach 74th Street. Turn right on 74th and head east one block, to the east side of Third Avenue.

13. J.G. Melon. 1291 Third Avenue (at 74th Street). After Jane had blown them off to go on her date, Charlie (Taylor Nichols), Tommy (Edward Clements) and Fred (Bryan Leder) came here to drink, smoke and gripe about the breakdown in their friendship that such an act of treason on Jane's part signified, in *Metropolitan.*

Continue east on 74th Street to Second Avenue. Cross Second and stop in front of the first building on the southeast corner of 74th Street and Second Avenue.

14. 300 East 74th Street (at Second Avenue). There was a madman on the loose, committing acts of pure evil with the help of a hammer. But Detective Ed Delaney (Frank Sinatra) was on the case and his research, his leads and his hunches led him to this building, where he convinced a doorman to give him access to the serial killer's apartment, in *The First Deadly Sin.*

Return to Second Avenue, turn right, and walk north the three blocks to the north side of 77th Street. Turn right on 77th and stop in front of 325 East 77th.

15. 325 East 77th Street. Five years after the ghosts, ghouls and other slobbering demons had invaded her last apartment (see *Manhattan on Film*, **Walking Tour 2**, Location 10), Dana Barrett (Sigourney Weaver) had decided to relocate. But she didn't get far enough away. At the beginning of *Ghostbusters II*, Dana was returning to her home in this building when the demons struck again, propelling her baby carriage down the street and out into traffic. Dana gave chase onto First Avenue and luckily, the baby was unhurt. But she knew that she had no choice but to reestablish contact with the zany Ghostbusters, as well as her past.

Follow Dana's baby's carriage to First Avenue, turn left on First and walk north. At 84th Street, note the building diagonally across First, on the northeast corner of First and 84th.

16. 401 East 84th Street. He was a good cop, but when his partner was killed leaving three kids without a dad, Artie Lewis (Michael

Keaton) decided he had to take matters into his own hands. After following Grace (Rachel Ticotin) here, Artie donned a ski mask, tricked his way into the apartment of the drug dealer with whom Grace was involved and took away their loot. Artie was no longer such a good cop, but he had his reasons for what he did. And so did Grace, who wasn't quite what she appeared to be, either, in *One Good Cop*.

Continue up First to 87th Street and turn left. Walk west one block to Second Avenue, and note the building on the west side of the street, between 87th and 88th Streets.

17. 245 East 87th Street. He could come and go as he pleased, but Mel (Jack Lemmon) felt like a prisoner nonetheless. It was hot outside, he had lost his job, his apartment was burglarized and he never seemed to have exact change for the bus. Mel was a *Prisoner of Second Avenue*, and he lived in this building with his wife Edna (Anne Bancroft), who had her share of bad days here too.

Tour 5

Head north on Second Avenue one block, until you are across from Elaine's, the legendary literary hotspot, between 88th and 89th Streets.

18. Elaine's. 1703 Second Avenue (between 88th and 89th Streets). Seeking a night of culture after many nights stuck in with the kids, playwright Ivan Travalian (Al Pacino) and his new girlfriend Alice Detroit (Dyan Cannon) went to a Roumanian film, then stopped in here to mix and mingle with the literary world, in *Author! Author!*

They worked together and there was a mutual attraction, but when they came here for a late dinner, they both knew they were heading down a dangerous path, since Max Schumacher (William Holden) was married. And sure enough, Max's dinner with Diane Christensen (Faye Dunaway) led to a torrid yet short-lived affair, in *Network*.

Book parties are a very frequent occurrence at Elaine's, and fittingly enough, a book party was held in *Celebrity* to celebrate "the best book ever written about the CIA."

You have now reached the end of **Walking Tour 5: The Inland Express**.

Walking Tour 6

Central Park

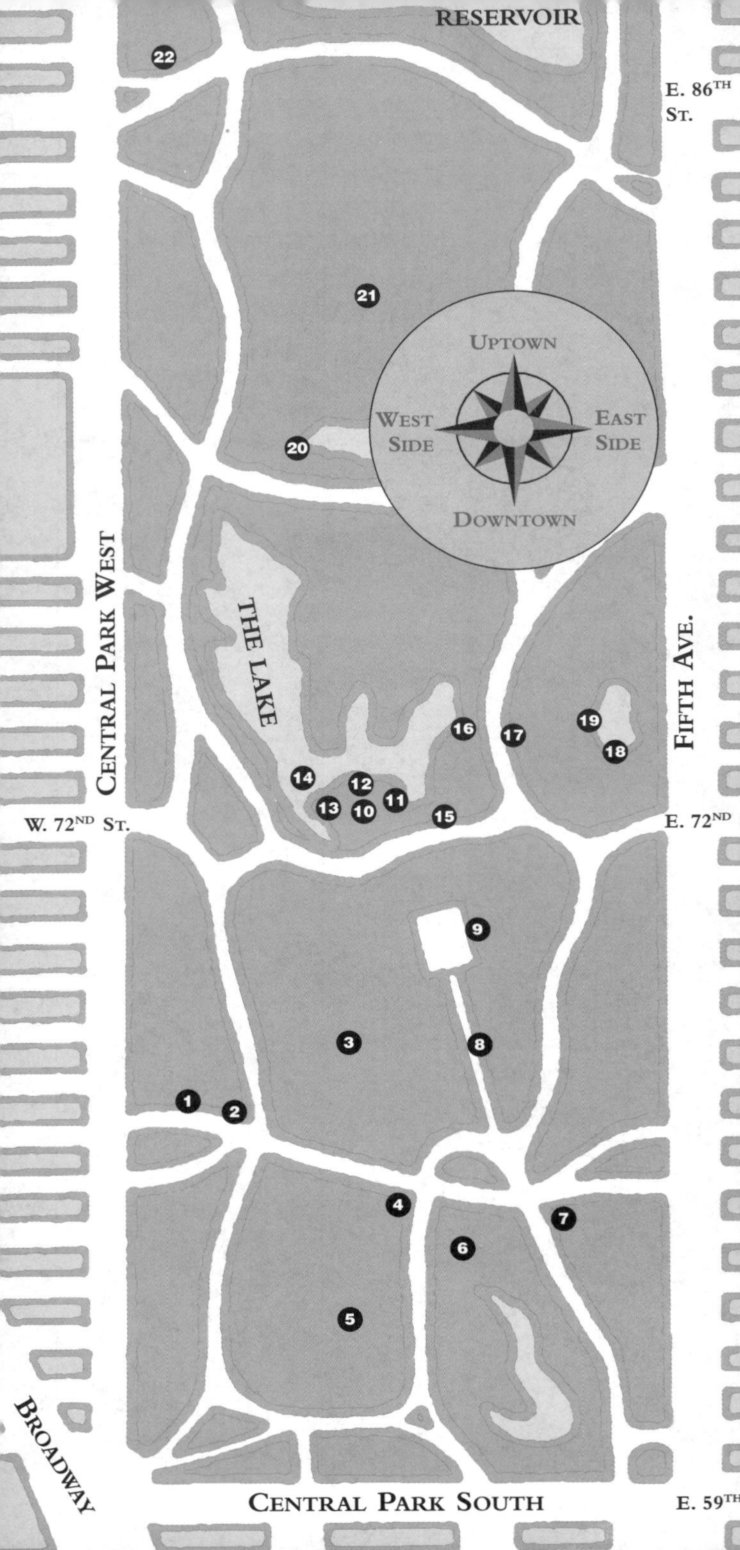
RESERVOIR
E. 86TH ST.
UPTOWN
WEST SIDE
EAST SIDE
DOWNTOWN
THE LAKE
CENTRAL PARK WEST
FIFTH AVE.
W. 72ND ST.
E. 72ND ST
BROADWAY
CENTRAL PARK SOUTH
E. 59TH
22
21
20
16
17
19
18
14
12
13
10
11
15
9
3
8
1
2
4
7
6
5

Walking Tour 6

CENTRAL PARK

A beautiful example of the marriage of nature and design, Central Park is for visitors one of the most unexpected treasures of New York. Most people from elsewhere only hear horror stories about this New York City gem and believe it to be one of the most dangerous places on earth, but nothing could be further from the truth. Hopefully, a brief trip through Central Park should convince the TourWalker of its beauty and abundance of pleasures.

Walking Tour 6: Central Park begins at Tavern on the Green, just east of Central Park West and 66th Street. If you choose to get to the starting point by public transportation, you may use any of these subway or bus lines (but the following list is by no means exhaustive):

FROM THE NORTH

SUBWAYS

- **1** or **2** southbound to 66th Street. Walk east on 66th to Central Park West.
- **B** or **C** southbound to 72nd Street. Walk south on Central Park West to 66th Street.

BUSES

- **M5** southbound on Riverside Drive, then Broadway, to 66th Street. Walk east on 66th to Central Park West.
- **M7** southbound on Columbus Avenue to 66th Street. Walk east on 66th to Central Park West.

- **M10** southbound on Central Park West to 66th Street.
- **M104** southbound on Broadway to 66th Street. Walk east on 66th to Central Park West.

FROM THE SOUTH

SUBWAYS

- **1** or **2** northbound to 66th Street. Walk east on 66th to Central Park West.
- **A**, **B**, **C** or **D** northbound to 59th Street/Columbus Circle. Walk north on Central Park West to 66th Street.

BUSES

- **M5** or **M7** northbound on Avenue of the Americas to 59th Street, then westbound on 59th to Columbus Circle and north on Broadway to 66th Street. Walk east on 66th to Central Park West.
- **M10** northbound on Hudson Street, then Eighth Avenue, then Central Park West, to 66th Street.
- **M104** northbound on Eighth Avenue, then Broadway, to 66th Street. Walk east on 66th to Central Park West.

FROM THE EAST

SUBWAYS

- **7** or **42nd Street Shuttle** to Times Square. Transfer to **1** or **2** northbound to 66th Street. Walk east on 66th to Central Park West.

BUSES

- **M31** or **M57** westbound on 57th Street to Eighth Avenue. Transfer to the **M10** bus (or walk) north on Central Park West, to 66th Street.
- **M72** westbound to Central Park West and 66th Street.

FROM THE WEST

Buses

- **M31** or **M57** eastbound on 57th Street to Eighth Avenue. Transfer to the **M10** bus (or walk) north on Central Park West, to 66th Street.
- **M72** eastbound to Central Park West, then southbound on Central Park West to 66th Street.

However you choose to get to Central Park West and 66th Street, once you are there, walk east into the park through the entranceway to Tavern on the Green. A parking lot should be on your right. Stop when the restaurant's entrance comes into view.

1. Tavern on the Green. Just off Central Park West and 66th Street. In the original version of the movie, Jack Lemmon and Sandy Dennis spent a harrowing night in Central Park, and were not feeling all that romantic at the end of the day. In the remake, Steve Martin and Goldie Hawn took a break from their "nightmare" to rekindle their passion, only to have it come back to haunt them. In *The Out-of-Towners*, Henry (Steve Martin) and Nancy (Goldie Hawn) got kicked out of a cab that was being used as a getaway car by some criminals. They found themselves in Central Park and found a nice section of

Tour 6

grass to spend a few quiet, romantic, "private" moments together. But they were grossly mistaken. The "isolated" area turned out to be right outside this restaurant, and the lights were off only until Mayor Rudy Guiliani gave the word to turn them on as part of a "Light up the City" campaign. The Mayor and hundreds of prominent guests were inside Tavern on the Green, and when the lights went on, those assembled got a pretty revealing glimpse of Henry and Nancy.

Now close your eyes and count to three. When you open them, pretend that we have traveled back in time nearly half a century.

2. The Central Park Casino. Site of Tavern on the Green. On the spot now occupied by Tavern on the Green, Eddy Duchin (Tyrone Power) showed up for work at what was then the Central Park Casino. It wasn't a gambling mecca, but a restaurant and nightclub all rolled into one. But when he showed up for work, he learned that the job he expected to have with Leo Reisman's orchestra did not exist. And then Marjorie Oelrich (Kim Novak) stepped in, used her influence, and Eddy got the job and, as is so often the case, the girl. It was quite a story; it was *The Eddy Duchin Story*.

Continue past Tavern on the Green and, when traffic permits, cross Park Drive West until you reach the fence abutting Sheep Meadow. Turn right and follow the fence to its southern boundary, then turn left and head east, keeping Sheep Meadow on your left. As you walk, picture the park on a moonlit, summer night.

3. Central Park at Night. It was clearly filmed on a sound stage, but there was no mistaking the fact that the setting was intended to be Central Park. In *The Band Wagon*, Tony (Fred Astaire) and

Gabrielle (Cyd Charisse) started out as feuding co-stars, but gradually warmed to one another. In a magical and romantic scene that showcased the best New York has to offer and the wonder of Central Park, the two of them took a horse-drawn carriage ride through the park. At some point, they got out of the carriage, strutted their stuff to the classic "Dancing in the Dark," then gracefully got back in the carriage and, holding hands, headed off into the night.

Continue in the same direction until just before you reach the road. Turn right on the path and then make another quick right and walk down the path (the Playmates Arch will be on your left) until you reach the Carousel.

4. Central Park Carousel. Margaret (Barbra Streisand) had tried to tell her husband Paul (David Selby) that she was pregnant when she visited him at work (see **Walking Tour 3**, Location 1), but never got the chance. Subsequently, in *Up the Sandbox*, she found a note he left for her and came here to find him riding the Carousel with their kids. In a setting devoted to kids, she finally got to tell Paul that another child was heading their way.

Continue past the Carousel, taking the path

Tour 6

that forks to the left. When you reach the next path, you will turn left, but first, notice the playground the short distance in front of you.

5. Heckscher Playground. Central Park. He had always had a pretty distant relationship with his son, who often addressed him as sir. But after the boy's mother passed away, Eddy Duchin (Tyrone Power) did his best to play a larger role in the boy's life. He made some headway, but he, too, was dying, and he knew the time had come to tell young Peter (Rex Thompson) that his father would be going away again, this time for good. In *The Eddy Duchin Story*, father and son held that difficult conversation while Peter sat on the swing, in the playground before you.

Now turn left and head toward and through Driprock Arch. When you emerge on the other side, continue along the path that leads you directly to Wollman Rink.

6. Wollman Rink. While Jackie (Susan Sarandon) skated with her kids on the ice, soon-to-be *Stepmom* Isabel (Julia Roberts) snapped photographs so they would have a pictorial history of their time together. Initially troubled by her ex-husband's relationship with the much younger woman, Jackie warmed to the woman who would soon take her place when she realized that her health would not let her take care of the kids much longer.

When I learn that my days are numbered, I'm going white water rafting in Costa Rica. If I'm not up for that, maybe I'll take one of those hot air balloons over the Grand Canyon. And if I'm in really rough shape, I'll settle for a three-day binge in Las Vegas. Anything but ice-skating. What is it about the rink that makes people who are very sick want to fritter away so many of their dwindling supply of precious moments on the ice?

Jackie did it in *Stepmom*. So did Charlotte (Winona Ryder), in *Autumn in New York* (see **Walking Tour 8**, Location 26).

And in *Love Story*, Jenny (Ali MacGraw), weakened by her illness, sat on the bleachers and watched as her husband, Oliver (Ryan O'Neal), skated on this rink for the both of them. And when the skating was over, they sipped their hot chocolates in the little café inside and then headed straight for the hospital, where Jenny would spend her remaining days.

But the ice plays host to happy times as well. On a wondrous night, a night when New York never looked so good, a night that Jonathan (John Cusack) admitted was rapidly climbing up the charts on his list of best nights of his life, a long night filled with endless promise, a night that he and Sara (Kate Beckinsale) both wished could have gone on forever, the two of them came here to skate after meeting at a department store counter (see **Walking Tour 5**, Location 8) and sharing scrumptious desserts (see **Walking Tour 5**, Location 9). Jonathan hoped their night could turn into something more, but Sara preferred to leave it to chance. It would be many years before they would learn whether such a gamble would pay off, in *Serendipity*.

Head up the path to the north side of Wollman

Rink toward the Dairy, the small cottage-like building just beyond the patch of grass before you. When you reach the Dairy, turn right and follow the path up the hill to Park Drive East. Watch for passing cars.

7. Park Drive East, just east of The Dairy. He had done a horrible thing, motivated by appallingly *Cruel Intentions*. Having almost lost the ability to care for another, Sebastian (Ryan Phillippe) had turned on the charm to Annette (Reese Witherspoon), a self-proclaimed virgin who was to attend his prep school in the fall, and convinced her to sleep with him. And then the unexpected happened. Although he dumped her soon afterwards, Sebastian realized that he had actually fallen in love with her. But convincing her would be difficult, so he set out to find her. After a scuffle between Sebastian and Ronald (Sean Patrick Thomas), who did his best to avenge Annette's shabby treatment, Annette fell in the road here and Sebastian pushed her out of the way of an oncoming taxi. Having stolen her heart, he saved her life, losing his own in the process.

Cross Park Drive East, turn left and walk north until you reach the first set of traffic lights. Cross the road at the crosswalk and pass the statue of William Shakespeare. Bear to the right and walk along the long stretch known as The Mall, under the overhanging trees.

8. The Mall. His wife Patsy (Marcia Rodd) met with a violent death at the hand of a crazed gunman, and eccentric photographer Alfred (Elliott Gould) tried hard to make sense of it all. At the end of *Little Murders*, he wandered around with his camera, taking pictures of anything and everything, some of which were of people walking and hanging out along The Mall.

Alfred probably missed Sonny (Adam Sandler)

and Kevin (Jon Stewart) as they walked along The Mall in *Big Daddy*. While Kevin was overseas, Sonny had tried to adopt a young boy who showed up at the apartment he shared with Kevin, only to learn that Kevin was the boy's natural father. As they walked under this tree-lined promenade, Sonny imparted his child-caring wisdom to Kevin.

Continue north on The Mall until you reach the Bandshell at the northern tip of The Mall.

9. Bandshell. They were vagabonds, hippies, flower-children, practitioners of free love, products of the psychedelic 60s that protested the war in Vietnam and they did their best to spread love, cheer and flowers, all the while singing and dancing their way through life. All that activity is exhausting, however, and the exuberant youth from *Hair* spent the night sprawled out on stage in the Bandshell, catching up on their sleep.

Walk north, keeping the Bandshell on your right. Descend the first staircase you come to and walk through the archway until you emerge on Bethesda Terrace, near Bethesda Fountain.

10. Bethesda Fountain. As Police Commissioner, Anthony Russell (Henry Fonda) had sworn to defend and protect the citizens of New York. As part of his duties, Russell attended a meeting held near Bethesda Fountain on behalf of the City and the Police Athletic League. After the meeting, in *Madigan*, Commissioner Russell offered to walk one of the meeting's attendees, Mrs. Bentley (Susan Clark) to her next destination, a nearby department store. But during their stroll, it became apparent that although Russell was keeping New York safe, he was aiding and abetting Mrs. Bentley in her commission of adultery.

At the start of another movie that was mostly singing and dancing, the rag-tag group of fun-loving disciples in *Godspell* dropped what they had been doing and converged on the fountain, where they splashed and sang to their hearts' content.

If the foot traffic is not too great, you may wander around Bethesda Terrace surrounding Bethesda Fountain and view the pristine setting from different angles.

11. Bethesda Terrace. Mel (Jack Lemmon) had taken about as much as he was willing to take, and he refused to take any more. He lost his job, had no air conditioning in his apartment and was just plain fed up. And after a man (future box office superstar Sylvester Stallone) bumped into Mel on Fifth Avenue, Mel noticed his wallet was missing. Assuming that the man had lifted his wallet, Mel chased him into Central Park, across Bethesda Terrace and back out of the park where he finally retrieved his wallet. Mel was a victim, *The Prisoner of Second Avenue*, but the wallet he recovered wasn't his own: it belonged to the poor man he had chased. Another example of how nothing went right for Mel.

As you walk around the terrace, however, watch out for people whizzing by on their in-line skates. One such skater was Charlie (Nicolas Cage), who celebrated winning the lottery by going skating with Yvonne (Bridget Fonda), a waitress with whom he had agreed to share his winnings. But in *It Could Happen to You*, he was a better cop and person than he was a skater, and Yvonne watched as Charlie, unable to stop, skated through the terrace and into the lake.

While facing the lake (Bethesda Fountain should be behind you), turn left and exit Bethesda Terrace on the path. Follow the path around as it curves to the right, keeping the lake on your right. Stop when you get a good view of the lake.

12. Path Just South of the Lake. They once nearly had a fling, but had gone their own ways when their careers took them in separate directions. Now the old gang was reuniting in New York for a friend's wedding, and soon-to-be-published author Harper (Taye Diggs) reminisced with the beautiful Jordan (Nia Long) as they walked down a path alongside this lake, in *The Best Man*. The wedding would be threatened when news surfaced that Harper actually had a fling with the bride-to-be, but the afternoon by the lake was still a peaceful and friendly one.

Walk a bit in the same direction, then look up at the hill to your left, overlooking the lake.

13. Cherry Hill. Overlooking the Lake. Not really sure why, literary agent Martha Marie Talridge (Demi Moore) accepted the invitation of Aaron Riley (William Fichtner) to join him at 9:00 o'clock on a Sunday morning. He supplied the coffee and the two of them sat on the grass overlooking the lake, and talked. He told her he was interested in her and in who she was, but

Martha herself wasn't even sure which of her two lives—the high-powered New York literary agent or the single mother in a tranquil European town—was real and which was a dream, in *Passion of Mind*.

Spotting Layla (Joey Lauren Adams) near the lake, Sonny (Adam Sandler) enlisted the help of young Julian (Cole and Dylan Sprouse) to win a date with the attorney, in *Big Daddy*.

Turn back and head east on the same path, keeping the lake on your left. If there's a rowboat out on the water, focus on it, and pretend.

14. Rowboat on The Lake. Their first meeting had ended in disaster, with each sneaking out of the restaurant when the other wasn't looking. But on a particular *Sunday in New York*, when Eileen (Jane Fonda) and Mike (Rod Taylor) ran into each other a short time later, they realized that maybe they should give it another shot. So the two of them came here and took a boat out onto the lake, starting the getting-acquainted process for real.

But while Mike did the rowing for Eileen, Hubbell Gardner (Robert Redford) had no such illusions of chivalry. While he relaxed at one end of the boat, Katie (Barbra Streisand) did the rowing of their boat on this same body of water, in *The Way We Were*.

Early in their relationship, New York restaurateur Will (Richard Gere) and the much younger Charlotte (Winona Ryder) strolled along Bow Bridge, which crosses over the lake, in *Autumn in*

New York. By the end of the film, much had changed and seasons had come and gone. A lonelier, but more mature Will sat in a rowboat on the lake with his daughter and grandchild and glanced at the bridge, remembering his autumn days with Charlotte.

Continue along the path until you re-emerge on Bethesda Terrace. Cross the terrace and find the path on the other side that leads toward the Boathouse Café, to your left. But before taking the path, turn back and note the staircase to the left of the archway that descends to Bethesda Terrace from the 72nd Street Transverse above.

15. Eastern Staircase to Bethesda Terrace. Ben Marco (Frank Sinatra) knew that something had gone terribly wrong for Raymond Shaw (Laurence Harvey), in *The Manchurian Candidate*. Ever since they came back from the war, Raymond was a changed man, and Ben was intent on finding out how, and why. One day, Ben followed Raymond through Central Park and watched as Raymond descended this staircase and jumped into the lake. He realized that such behavior did not bode well for the future, but it would still be a while before Ben learned exactly what that future was intended to be.

Turn to the left and head along the path you are on. Turn right when you reach the staircase that leads down away from the lake. Descend the staircase until just before the bottom.

16. Staircase near Boathouse Café. During his long and illustrious career, Jack Lemmon probably spent more time near Bethesda Terrace than almost any other actor, which is surprising, since Central Park has not always treated him well. Although he met a neighbor and future love interest near Bethesda Terrace in *It Should*

Happen to You (see *Manhattan on Film*, **Walking Tour 6**, Location 11), most of his memories of this part of New York were not good ones. As noted in Location 11, above, Bethesda Terrace was where he chased Sylvester Stallone, whom he suspected of having stolen his wallet, in *The Prisoner of Second Avenue*. Down this staircase, only a few yards from the terrace, Lemmon found himself in more trouble, once again at the hands of Neil Simon. In *The Out of Towners*,

Lemmon played George, a man who had come to New York to interview for a job. When he and his wife Gwen (Sandy Dennis) were turned away from their hotel, which had given away their room (see **Walking Tour 5**, Location 1), the two of them spent a harrowing night in Central Park, battling the elements, as well as a shoe thief. The next morning, famished, they still had one more battle to wage: fighting off a stray dog for the few remaining morsels in a box of Cracker Jacks they had found. Victorious at last, George and Gwen sat at the base of these stairs and ate the few pieces of candy-coated popcorn.

Leaving the steps and the lake behind, pass through Trefoil Arch and when you emerge on the other side, turn back and face the arch you just left.

17. Trefoil Arch. Just east of Boathouse Café. In unfamiliar territory, psychiatrist Dr. Sam Rice (Roy Scheider) followed someone he thought was Brooke Reynolds (Meryl Streep) and got mugged underneath this arch. Knowing that a mugger was the least of his worries in *Still of the Night*, Dr. Rice asked the mugger to look out for him until he got safely out of the park, but the man did not honor the request, and Dr. Rice lost his coat in the process.

Make your way along the path that leads from Trefoil Arch until you reach the Sailboat Pond, near the eastern border of the park.

18. Sailboat Pond. They attended the same school, but their friendship was just beginning. Their world was about to merge with someone else's, but first, they had to get to know each other. One Saturday morning, in *The World of Henry Orient*, Marion Gilbert (Merrie Spaeth) and Valerie Boyd (Tippy Walker) arranged to

meet at the Sailboat Pond and go adventuring, which involved spying on people, usually from a safe perch.

Turn to your left and stand before the statue of Hans Christian Anderson.

19. Statue of Hans Christian Anderson, by Sailboat Pond. Upon first learning that he had a son, options trader Michael Cromwell (Tim Allen) didn't think they would ever get along. While Cromwell made his living in the financial jungle, his son Mimi Siku (Sam Huntington) lived in a real jungle, half a world away. But after spending some time together, Cromwell realized that having a son was pretty cool. In *Jungle 2 Jungle*, father and son joined a crowd and danced in front of this statue to the strains of live music, something Michael never would have done before.

Turn right and walk along, keeping the Sailboat Pond to your right. Make a left on the first path you come to and walk west, following the path as it slopes up to Park Drive East. Cross the road when a safe opportunity presents itself, turn right and follow the road as it bends to the left, then to the right. You will see a sign for the "Belvedere Castle Nature Center." Head left and follow the path indicated by the sign (the path goes up, then down). Pass the statue of King Jagiello and follow the path until you reach the Great Lawn. Turn to the left and get a good look at Belvedere Castle, on the hilltop just to the south and west of the Great Lawn.

20. Belvedere Castle. She wasn't their mom, but Isabel (Julia Roberts) should have been paying closer attention, especially since she would soon be their *Stepmom*. While Isabel filmed an ad at Belvedere Castle, the kids waited nearby. But soon they had trouble locating Ben (Liam Aiken) and Isabel searched frantically in and around the castle. Luckily for Isabel and her future with Ben's father Luke (Ed Harris), Ben was finally found.

Follow the path that keeps Belvedere Castle to your left and the Great Lawn to your right. While you walk west, let your eyes wander along the vast expanse that is the Great Lawn.

21. The Great Lawn. Helene (Anne Bancroft) loved books but had trouble finding them in bookshops in New York. Luckily for Helene, there was a bookstore at *84 Charing Cross Road*, in London, that was able to send her whatever books she desired. One of her favorite pastimes was to walk in the park along portions of the Great Lawn and read the books she received.

Continue in the same direction and stay on the path as it slopes down to Park Drive West. Turn right on the side of the road and walk north until you reach 86th Street. Cross the road and head for the exit to the park near Central Park West and 86th Street, but before you leave the park, turn to the right and survey the plot of grass just before you.

22. Field just off Central Park West at 86th Street. Lance Barton (Chris Rock) had lost his body in a heavenly mishap, but was given a temporary one, that of millionaire Charles Wellington, to occupy, in *Down to Earth*. Although Lance found it difficult to woo the woman of his dreams while in the body of an old middle aged white man, he gamely did his best during an outing he sponsored for patients and staff of the Brooklyn County Hospital, held on this plot of land.

You have reached the end of **Walking Tour 6: Central Park**. If you continue west on the path you are on, you will exit the park on Central Park West and 86th Street.

Walking Tour 7

The Eastern Seaboard

EAST RIVER
E. 86TH ST.
UPTOWN
WEST SIDE
EAST SIDE
DOWNTOWN
EAST END AVE.
E. 72ND ST.
MADISON AVE.
PARK AVE.
LEXINGTON AVE.
THIRD AVE.
SECOND AVE.
FIRST AVE.
YORK AVE.
E. 59TH ST.
E. 42ND ST.
1
2
3
4
5
6
7
8
9
10
11
12
13
14
15
16
17
18
19
20
21

Walking Tour 7

The Eastern Seaboard

Manhattan is bordered on the east by the East River, along which some of the most elegant homes are located, and the people who live in them enjoy a scenic proximity to the river and a wealth of film locations all along Manhattan's eastern seaboard.

Walking Tour 7: The Eastern Seaboard begins on 42nd Street, between Second and Third Avenues, on the south side of the street. If you choose to get to the starting point by public transportation, you may use any of the following subway or bus lines (although the following list is by no means exhaustive):

FROM THE NORTH

SUBWAYS

- **4, 5 or 6** southbound to 42nd Street/Grand Central Station. Walk east on 42nd Street to 220 East 42nd (between Third and Second Avenues).

BUSES

- **M101, M102 or M103** southbound on Lexington Avenue to 42nd Street. Walk east on 42nd to 220 East 42nd (between Third and Second Avenues).

FROM THE SOUTH

SUBWAYS

- **1, 2, 3, N, R, Q or W** northbound to 42nd Street/Times Square. Transfer to **7** or **42nd Street Shuttle** eastbound to Grand Central

Station. Walk east on 42nd Street to 220 East 42nd.

- **4, 5** or **6** northbound to 42nd Street/Grand Central Station. Walk east on 42nd Street to 220 East 42nd.

Buses

- **M1** northbound on Park Avenue South, then Park Avenue, to 42nd Street. Walk east on 42nd to 220 East 42nd.
- **M101, M102** or **M103** northbound on Third Avenue to 42nd Street. Walk east on 42nd to 220 East 42nd.

FROM THE WEST

Subways

- **1, 2,** or **3** southbound to 42nd Street/Times Square. Transfer to **7** or **42nd Street Shuttle,** eastbound from Times Square to Grand Central Station. Walk east on 42nd Street to 220 East 42nd.

Buses

- **M42** eastbound on 42nd Street to Third Avenue. Walk east on 42nd to 220 East 42nd.
- **M104** southbound on Broadway, then eastbound on 42nd Street, to Third Avenue. Walk east on 42nd to 220 East 42nd.

However you choose to get to 220 East 42nd Street, when you get there, look up at The News Building towering above you.

1. The News Building. 220 East 42nd Street (between Second and Third Avenues). Although this building is called The News building and houses the New York paper known as the *Daily News*, in *Superman*, it housed the *Daily Planet*, the paper that employed Clark Kent, Lois Lane, Cub Reporter Jimmy Olson and gruff editor Perry White.

Head east until halfway between Second and

First Avenues. Ascend the staircase that leads to Tudor City. When you reach the top, continue east until you reach the railing overlooking First Avenue. You should have a clear view of the tall structure across the street, the United Nations Secretariat Building.

2. United Nations. Secretariat Building. The home of diplomacy and intrigue, often existing side by side, the United Nations was presided over by Secretary General Douglas Thomas (Donald Sutherland) and his assistant Eleanor (Anne Archer), in *The Art of War.* Some people inside the building's walls worked in favor of a trade agreement with China, and others wanted it scrapped. The trick lay in knowing who was on which side and it often fell to Neil Shaw (Wesley Snipes), who officially didn't even exist, but performed services on behalf of the United Nations, to keep things running smoothly.

To the right of the Secretariat Building, just south of 42nd Street, observe the playground in the shadows of the elevated FDR Drive, a short distance away, just east of you.

3. Robert Moses Playground. 42nd Street and FDR Drive. In her case, having *Love With the Proper Stranger* left Angela (Natalie Wood) pregnant. Not cut out to be a father, trumpet player Rocky (Steve McQueen) still wanted to do the right thing, which meant borrowing money from his parents to help Angela "take care of the problem." He brought her to this park, where his parents were spending the afternoon with friends, but when Angela's father and brothers showed up, Rocky grabbed her and they fled to the relative safety of a vacant building nearby.

Return to Tudor Place (the road just behind where you are standing) and turn right. Walk north and stop at the last building on the right.

4. 45 Tudor Place. Wesley Snipes worked for, and spent a good deal of time inside, the United Nations, in *The Art of War*. But in *U.S. Marshals*, he played Mark Sheridan, who came to New York to clear his name. The first thing he did was rent an apartment in this building, which offered an unimpeded view of the United Nations, across First Avenue.

Continue past 45 Tudor Place and turn right. If you pause at the fence, you may get yet another glimpse of the Secretariat Building. Descend the staircase to First Avenue. At the bottom (Ralph Bunche Park), turn left and walk north on First Avenue. When you reach 45th Street, turn and look at the General Assembly Building, the low building north of the Secretariat Building, across First Avenue from where you are standing.

5. United Nations. General Assembly Building. Having fled the clutches of the men who mistook him for a man named George Kaplan yet again, Roger Thornhill (Cary Grant) came here to find Lester Townsend, who worked for the organization known as Unipol. Roger had reason to believe that Townsend was connected to his kidnapping, but a few minutes later, Townsend (Philip Ober) lay dead with a knife in his back and Roger was the chief suspect in the murder. Heading *North By Northwest*, he was on the run again.

Continue north on First Avenue. At 49th Street, turn right and cross First, continuing east one block (up Mitchell Place) until you reach Beekman Place. Turn left and walk the short distance until you are in front of 3 Beekman Place (the door just north of One Beekman Place).

6. 3 Beekman Place. She coaxed the blues right out of the horn. She charmed the husk right off of the corn. Her name was Mame Dennis (Lucille Ball) and when her nephew Patrick (Bruce Davison) moved in, she became Auntie Mame. Together, as long as the money held out, Patrick and Auntie *Mame* lived here.

Continue to Beekman Place North (same as 51st Street), turn left and walk west until you return to First Avenue. Cross First, turn right and walk north until you reach the Metropolitan Café, at 959 First Avenue, just south of 53rd Street.

7. Metropolitan Café. 959 First Avenue (between 52nd and 53rd Streets). He had a small place in Brooklyn that he called his own, but Alby (Elliott Gould) aspired to make his mark in the restaurant world in Manhattan. With the help of his sophisticated, opinionated and meddling Uncle Benjamin (Sid Caesar), Alby had a chance to buy the restaurant that was located here, but his uncle's assistance came with significant strings attached. If Alby played by his uncle's rules, he would get his restaurant, in *Over the Brooklyn Bridge*, but he would have to give up control over his heart, and dump his non-Jewish girlfriend, a heavy price indeed.

Continue north to 55th Street, turn right and head east until you reach Sutton Place, one block east of First Avenue. Cross to the far side of Sutton Place and turn back to look at the building on the northwest corner of Sutton Place and 55th Street.

8. 36 Sutton Place South (at 55th Street). It was an event that made every single man (and plenty of married men) in New York jump for joy: three beautiful women moving to Manhattan and throwing themselves into New York's social scene. Pooling their resources, Shotzy (Lauren Bacall), Paula (Marilyn Monroe) and Loco (Betty Grable) decided to share a furnished apartment in this elegant building, selling off pieces of furniture as needed to pay their expenses. But it was all for a good cause: to find wealthy husbands, in *How to Marry a Millionaire.*

Walk north one block, to 56th Street, and turn right. Walk east as far as you can go.

9. Sutton Place and 56th Street. The Dead End sign says it all. It was clearly a set, but intended to depict life in this part of Manhattan. Right around here, a cop walked his beat, the rich people lived in the houses up above and looked down upon the street urchins and poor

working souls who inhabited the slums below, overlooking the East River. This was the world of *Dead End*, inhabited by Dave (Joel McCrae), an architect trying to earn a humble yet honest living, a young woman named Drina (Sylvia Sidney), who was doing her best to keep her kid brother from falling in with the wrong crowd, and Baby Face (Humphrey Bogart), who had no regard for decency, goodness or the law. It was also the place where the Dead End Kids (Leo Gorcey, Huntz Hall and Gabriel Dell, among others) got their start, and their name.

In more modern times, a moody writer named George Prager (Frank Langella) had an apartment right around here, with a breathtaking view of the river, in *Diary of a Mad Housewife*. Before long, he found himself in a relationship with a bored and unappreciated housewife, Tina Balser (Carrie Snodgrass), who visited him in his apartment on numerous occasions. For fans of Howard Stern, it may be interesting to note that, in this movie Frank Langella looked an awful lot like Howard Stern in his college and early radio days, as depicted in the movie *Private Parts*.

Return to Sutton Place, make a right and walk one block north to 57th Street. Turn right on 57th and walk to the railing overlooking the small playground down below.

10. Sutton Place and 57th Street. Playground Overlooking East River. Feeling depressed and unhappy, and wondering why she was wasting her time with a married man, Ellen Gordon (Jane Fonda) ran from her apartment (see **Walking Tour 5,** Location 10) and came here, a place she liked to visit when she needed to think. One time, Cass Henderson (Dean Jones) was in hot pursuit of her and finding her on the ledge, feared she would jump. But in *Any Wednesday*, ending it all was not what Ellen had in mind. And after she and Cass sat on the swings and talked, she decided the two of them should get married. Cass was flattered, since they had just met earlier in the day, but in New York anything is possible.

Another address doesn't exist, but if it did, it would be in one of the buildings near where you are now standing.

11. 600 East 57th Street. In his apartment that overlooked the East River and had a view of the 59th Street Bridge second to none, happy-go-lucky playboy Charlie Reader (Frank Sinatra) entertained a bevy of beauties who battled for his affections, in *The Tender Trap*. That is, until one of them, Julie Gillis (Debbie Reynolds), snared him in her own tender trap.

From this vantage point, you can get the same wonderful view of the 59th Street Bridge that Charlie Reader got from his living room window.

12. 59th Street Bridge. Wesley Snipes has made his share of New York movies, and interestingly enough, many of them have had scenes located along the East River. In *New Jack City*, Snipes played Nino Brown, a man with his fingers in a lot of different pots, none of them legal. As the movie opened, Nino emerged from a car on the 59th Street Bridge and stood by as one of his associates held a man upside down from the ankles, over the side of the bridge. The poor sap didn't have the money or the drugs that belonged to Nino, and he had to be taught a lesson. After Nino gave the word, the man was dropped into the waters of the East River below.

Although you cannot quite see it from here, imagine the plot of ground beginning under the Manhattan side of the bridge and extending a short distance north.

13. Under the 59th Street Bridge. He actually hailed from a prominent and well-to-do Boston family, but he found himself down on his luck. He was plucked from this location, where he had made a transient home with other forgotten men, only to find that life with the Bullock family, for whom he became the butler, was no picnic either. In *My Man Godfrey*, Godfrey (William Powell) taught the Bullocks about life and taught the young Irene Bullock (Carole Lombard) about love. And when Godfrey opened a gentleman's club on this site at the end of the movie, Irene stopped by to show him what she had learned about the subject.

Return to Sutton Place. Walk west on 57th Street until you reach the far side of First Avenue. Turn right on First and walk north to 59th Street. Turn left on 59th and stop in front of 346 East 59th Street, a short distance west from First Avenue.

14. 346 East 59th Street. It does not seem unusual for some movie locations to appear in more than one movie. Although a city like New York boasts thousands of buildings, restaurants, hotels and stores, some of the more prominent ones (*e.g.*, Tavern on the Green, the Waldorf-Astoria, Gray's Papaya) appear time and again. But I found it so surprising that the location before you has appeared in more than one film that I had to mention it here. In *Manhattan on Film*, I pointed out that this building was where Maria (Melanie Griffith) had an apartment in *Bonfire of the Vanities* (see *Manhattan on Film*, **Walking Tour 5**, Location 12). It is also where Felix (George Segal) and

Doris (Barbra Streisand) each had an apartment in *The Owl and the Pussycat*, until Felix got them evicted by complaining about Doris's nighttime habits.

Return to First Avenue. On the southeast corner of the intersection is another location from *The Owl and the Pussycat*.

15. 400 East 59th Street. Southeast Corner of 59th and First Avenue. Luckily for Felix and Doris, when they got evicted from the building you just left, they didn't have far to go to find a place to sleep. They crossed First Avenue and had the doorman ring up. Moments later, in *The Owl and the Pussycat*, Felix's friend and co-worker Barney (Robert Klein) was putting them up for the night at his apartment in this building.

Turn left and walk north on First Avenue to 69th Street. Turn right on 69th and walk east one block, to York Avenue. You should be standing across from the hospital.

16. New York Presbyterian Hospital—New York Weill Cornell Medical Center. 1300 York Avenue (at 69th Street). Connie (Kelly Lynch) worked here as a nurse. In *Three of Hearts*, she dreaded attending her younger sister's wedding without a date until one of her patients suggested that she rent a date through an escort service. And she did (William Baldwin).

If you wish to walk east to get a better glimpse of the promenade along the East River, you may do so. If not, I will tell you what you would see if you had.

17. East River Promenade. North and east of New York Hospital. He lost his first wife, and then fell in love with the woman who cared for his young son. But knowing he didn't have much time to live, Eddy Duchin (Tyrone Power) fled the home of his friends, the Wadsworths (see **Walking Tour 4**, Location 17), and came to the promenade along the river to clear his head. And

Tour 7

when the woman he loved, Chiquita (Victoria Shaw) followed him, he revealed his love for her, as well as the illness that would soon take his life. She then confessed her love for him and they agreed to marry, for however much time they had left together, in *The Eddy Duchin Story*.

If you walked east to the river, return to York Avenue and turn right. If you did not, turn left on York and in either case, walk north on York until you reach 77th Street. Turn right on 77th and walk east until you are in front of 523 East 77th Street.

18. 523 East 77th Street. Inside this elegant and majestic building, Lee Simon (Kenneth Branagh) attended a photo shoot, then stood out in the street polishing his snazzy car, in *Celebrity*. When a supermodel (Charlize Theron) walked out of the building, Lee offered her a ride and then spent a pretty hectic evening cavorting with the glamorous set, hoping it would give him an evening not to forget. It did. By the end of the evening, his car was a wreck and the supermodel left him to fend for himself.

Return to York Avenue. Turn right and walk north to 81st Street. Turn right on 81st and walk east until you are across from Le Boeuf a la Mode, at 539 East 81st Street.

19. Le Boeuf a la Mode. 539 East 81st Street. After getting suspended from the police force for using excessive force in the line of duty, Megan (Jamie Lee Curtis) left her precinct and found herself in a sudden downpour. With cabs scarce, she agreed to share a cab with Eugene (Ron Silver), never realizing he was the city's newest serial killer, in *Blue Steel*. With so much traffic they hardly moved and Eugene suggested they wait out the rain and traffic over dinner. They got out of the cab and came to this restaurant. The chocolate mousse alone warrants a visit.

Continue east on 81st Street until you reach the far side of East End Avenue. Turn left on East End Avenue and walk north to 83rd Street. Turn right on 83rd and walk the short distance until you are in front of the school located at 610 East 83rd Street.

20. 610 East 83rd Street. Their world eventually overlapped with that of concert pianist Henry Orient (Peter Sellers) but until that time and during the day, the world of Marion Gilbert (Merrie Spaeth) and Valerie Boyd (Tippy Walker) revolved around their school, which was located here, in *The World of Henry Orient*.

Return to East End Avenue, turn right and walk north to 89th Street. You should be in front of Gracie Mansion, the home of New York City's Mayor.

21. Gracie Mansion. In *The Taking of Pelham One, Two, Three*, the Mayor (Lee Wallace) was laid up with the flu, and the last thing he wanted was to have a situation to deal with. But after a subway train was hijacked, he did what he could from his bed inside his official residence, here.

And years later, in *Ghostbusters II*, the Ghostbusters paid a visit to the Mayor (David Margulies) to tell him they had discovered a river of evil under the streets of Manhattan. As before, the Mayor was none too happy to see them and even dismissed them with a wave of his hand. But also as before, as soon as he realized that they were speaking the truth, he knew they represented his and New York City's best, if not only, hope.

You have now reached the end of **Walking Tour 7: The Eastern Seaboard**.

BROADWAY

Walking Tour 8

The Broadway Beat

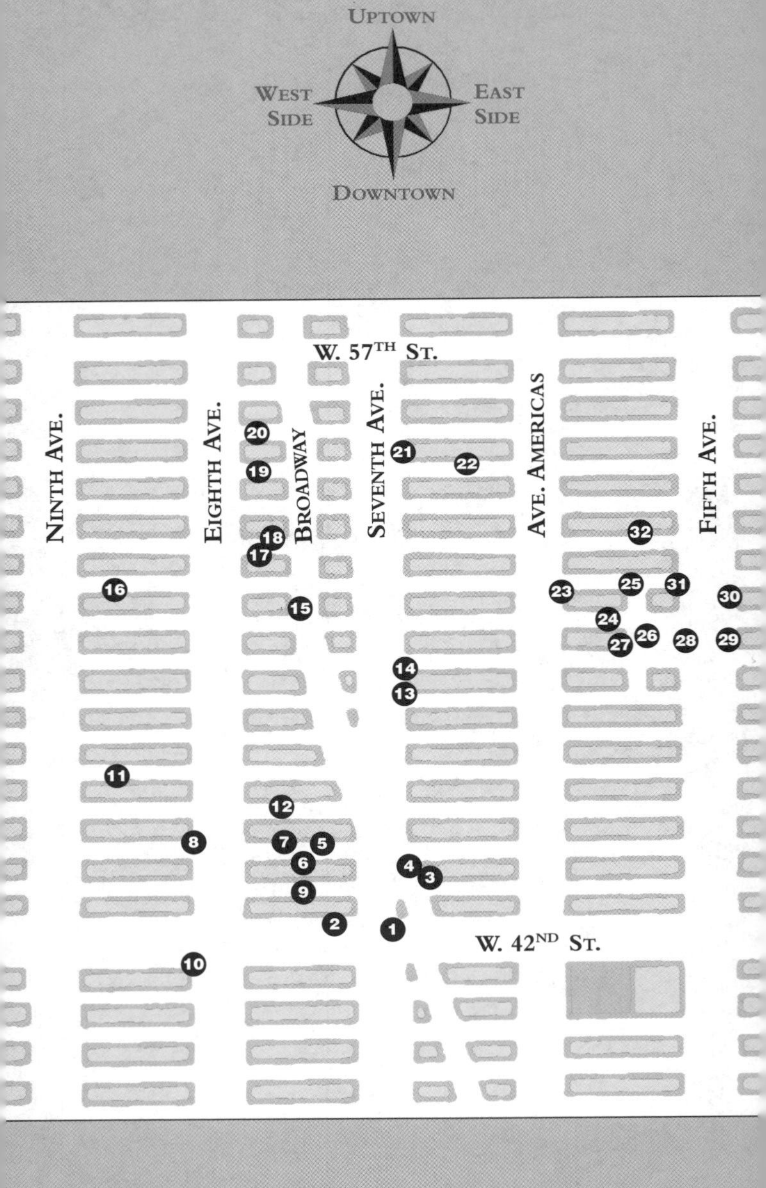

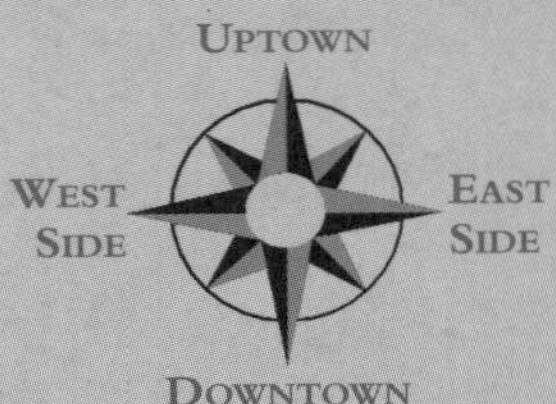

UPTOWN
WEST SIDE
EAST SIDE
DOWNTOWN
W. 57TH ST.
NINTH AVE.
EIGHTH AVE.
BROADWAY
SEVENTH AVE.
AVE. AMERICAS
FIFTH AVE.
W. 42ND ST.
1
2
3
4
5
6
7
8
9
10
11
12
13
14
15
16
17
18
19
20
21
22
23
24
25
26
27
28
29
30
31
32

Walking Tour 8

THE BROADWAY BEAT

A great cross-section of New York City's offerings can be found within the confines of **Walking Tour 8: The Broadway Beat**. From the thrill of a Broadway show, to the underbelly of some of the less reputable dance clubs, from restaurants where the glitterati mingle to the world's most famous ice skating rink. Whatever your tastes, whatever your inclinations, **Walking Tour 8** should entertain you during the next two hours.

Walking Tour 8: The Broadway Beat begins at the intersection of 42nd Street and Seventh Avenue, smack in the middle of what is known throughout the world as Times Square. If you choose to get to the starting point by public transportation, you may use any of the following subway or bus lines (although the following list is by no means exhaustive):

FROM THE NORTH

SUBWAYS

- **1, 2,** or **3** southbound to 42nd Street/Times Square.
- **A** southbound to 42nd Street and Eighth Avenue. Walk east on 42nd to Seventh Avenue.

BUSES

- **M7** southbound on Columbus Avenue, then Broadway, then Seventh Avenue, to 42nd Street.
- **M6** southbound on Seventh Avenue to 42nd Street.

- **M10**, **M20** or **M104** southbound on Broadway to 42nd Street.

FROM THE SOUTH

Subways

- **1**, **2**, or **3** northbound to 42nd Street/Times Square.
- **A**, **C** or **E** northbound to Eighth Avenue and 42nd Street. Walk east on 42nd to Seventh Avenue.
- **B**, **D**, **F**, **N**, **R** or **S** northbound to Sixth Avenue and 42nd Street. Walk west on 42nd to Seventh Avenue.
- **Q** or **W** northbound to 42nd Street/Times Square.

Buses

- **M5**, **M6** or **M7** northbound on Sixth Avenue to 42nd Street. Walk west on 42nd to Seventh Avenue.
- **M20** northbound on Hudson Street, then Eighth Avenue, to 42nd Street. Walk east on 42nd to Seventh Avenue.

FROM THE EAST

Subways

- **N** or **R** westbound, then southbound, to 42nd Street/Times Square.
- **Q** or **W** westbound, then southbound, to 42nd Street/Times Square.
- **7** or **42nd Street Shuttle** westbound to Times Square.

Buses

- **M42** or **M104** westbound on 42nd Street to Seventh Avenue.

FROM THE WEST

Buses

- **M42** eastbound on 42nd Street to Seventh Avenue.

Because Times Square is a general area, more than a specific location, get to the southwest corner of Seventh Avenue and 42nd Street. Then, before you go anywhere else, look all around and take in the splendor that is Times Square. Not quite as colorful as it was before its recent cleanup (the x-rated movie houses and porn palaces that had been ubiquitous for years have been relocated), the area still exemplifies the startling cultural diversity that can be found by walking a block in any direction.

1. Times Square. Sky Masterson, Nathan Detroit, Big Jule, Nicely Nicely Johnson, Sister Sarah Brown, Miss Adelaide and her Hot Box Girls, Benny Southstreet, Harry the Horse. Even the names evoke a different era: a time of shady charmers, irreverent gamblers and irrepressible dreamers. They wore bright-colored suits, spit-shined shoes and bet on everything from sales of cheesecake to whether a certain guy could take a certain doll to Havana. This was the world created by Damon Runyan, and Times Square was where the people who gave life to *Guys and Dolls* spent their long days and endless nights.

Without taking a step, focus on the New Amsterdam Theater, located across 42nd Street from where you are standing.

2. New Amsterdam Theater. 214 West 42nd Street. The theater may be newly renovated but it has been around a long time. In Broadway's earlier days, when great showmen and impresarios ruled the night, the original New Amsterdam Theater was where Flo Ziegfeld (Willaim Powell), in *The Great Ziegfeld*, staged many of his great "Follies."

Cross 42nd Street and walk north on Seventh Avenue, one block. Turn to the right and look at

1500 Broadway, at the northeast corner of Broadway and 43rd Street.

3. 1500 Broadway. Northeast Corner of Broadway and 43rd Street. Tabloid TV has always flirted with crossing the line of decency, but in *15 Minutes*, it actually crossed over to the other side. From his studio, which was located in this building, tabloid TV anchor Robert Hawkins (Kelsey Grammar) aired his exclusive footage of the brutal and heinous torture and subsequent execution of Detective Eddie Flemming (Robert De Niro) at the hands of publicity-seeking, camera-toting terrorists. Irate over the airing of the tragedy, police stormed the building.

As you look across Seventh Avenue and Broadway, look for a muscular man, wearing a toga and driving a chariot down Seventh Avenue.

4. Seventh Avenue and 43rd Street. He was far from home and his English was non-existent, which makes sense, since he hailed from Olympus and his voice was dubbed, but when Hercules (Arnold Strong, a.k.a. Mr. Universe, a.k.a. Arnold Schwarzenegger) was set loose in New York, anything was possible. In *Hercules in New York*, Hercules commandeered a horse-drawn carriage, turned it into a chariot and the chase was on, all around New York and just past the intersection you are looking at now.

Continue north on Seventh Avenue and turn left on 44th Street. Head west until you are across from the Shubert Theatre, at 225 West 44th Street.

5. Shubert Theatre. 225 West 44th Street. Every Broadway star wants fans, but nobody wants *The Fan*. And that's exactly what Sally Ross (Lauren Bacall) had. She was starring in a play called "Never Say Never" and Douglas

Breen (Michael Biehn) was making his move. He had wounded and killed to get close to her, and after the curtain had come down and the Shubert Theatre had emptied, it was just the two of them in a game of cat and mouse. But Sally was tough, and her number one fan would soon learn who was the mouse and who was the cat.

Continue west until you reach Sardi's, the legendary Broadway eatery.

6. Sardi's. 234 West 44th Street. Sardi's has traditionally been the place where those involved in Broadway opening nights come to party and wait for the first reviews of the shows to hit the newsstands. In *Forever Female*, that is exactly what people did while waiting for word on what the critics thought of the new show, "No Laughing Matter." Sardi's was used several times in the movie, and in one scene, after the show, aging star Beatrice Page (Ginger Rogers) was ushered in to the restaurant, to enjoy dinner with both her ex-husband and her current boyfriend George, played by George Reeves (Superman, in the classic television series).

Several decades later, Playwright Ivan Travalian (Al Pacino) came here with his kids, as well as the producer, cast and crew to await the reviews of his new show, "English With Tears."

It was worth the wait, for the reviews made them all smile, in *Author! Author!*

The Broadhurst Theater should be directly across the street.

7. Broadhurst Theater. 235 West 44th Street. He thought it was just a typical day, until some pretty bizarre things started happening to him. Before long, he was uttering thoughts that weren't his own and doing things he didn't want to do. He was John Malkovich, but that was proving to be not that uncommon, because in *Being John Malkovich*, countless others were paying good money to live his life. There was a bright side to all the disruption, however. During a rehearsal at this theater for the play in which he was appearing, Maxine (Catherine Keener) showed up and took John into his dressing room, where they engaged in a little afternoon delight.

Continue west on 44th Street until you reach Eighth Avenue. Look to the northwest corner of the intersection of 44th and Eighth.

8. Eighth Avenue and 44th Street. Northwest corner. It was just another crazy night in the life of paramedic Frank Pierce (Nicolas

Cage). Responding to a call in *Bringing Out the Dead*, Frank showed up here and found a crazy man named Noel (Marc Anthony) threatening to shove a broken bottle into his own neck. Luckily Frank talked him out of it.

Turn left and walk south on Eighth Avenue. At 43rd Street, turn left and walk east the short distance until you are across from the Hotel Carter, at 250 West 43rd Street.

9. Hotel Carter. 250 West 43rd Street. It was a far cry from the dilapidated mansion in Florida, but this was what Finn (Ethan Hawke) called home when he moved to New York, in *Great Expectations*.

Head back west on 43rd. At Eighth Avenue, turn left and look at the Port Authority Bus Terminal, on Eighth Avenue and 42nd Street.

10. Port Authority Bus Terminal. One of the major transportation hubs in Manhattan and one of the busiest bus stations in the world, this is where Florence Keefer (Judy Holliday) came with her daughter, in *The Marrying Kind*. The two of them boarded a bus bound for the town of Brewster, New York.

Cross Eighth Avenue, turn right and walk north to 46th Street. Turn left on 46th and walk west until you are in front of Joe Allen Restaurant, another timeless Broadway institution, at 326 West 46th Street.

11. Joe Allen Restaurant. 326 West 46th Street. Fresh out of rehab, Georgia (Marsha Mason) was hoping to make a new beginning, having finally put her alcoholic days behind her. But things got off to a rocky start when her ex, David (David Dukes) called her and asked her to meet him here. Over what both of them hoped would be a pleasant dinner, David revealed that he had written a play about their life together, and it was going to be produced. Georgia was less than thrilled and her mood turned even darker when, in *Only When I Laugh*, David said that he wanted her to star in the play, as herself.

Turn back and return to the east side of Eighth Avenue. Turn right on Eighth and walk south one block to 45th Street. Turn left on 45th and stop in front of the Music Box Theater, at 239 West 45th Street.

12. Music Box Theater. 239 West 45th Street. They were sleuths, not very good ones, but they gave it their all. During a matinee performance of a show, Charlie (John Ritter) and Arthur (Blaine Novak) staked out the front of this theater, waiting for the people they had been hired to follow, to exit the building, in *They All Laughed*.

Continue east on 45th Street. Cross Broadway and Seventh Avenue, which converge almost at the very point where you are. When you reach the far side of Seventh Avenue, turn left and walk north on Seventh until you reach 723 Seventh Avenue, which is just north of 48th Street.

13. 723 Seventh Avenue (between 48th and 49th Streets). In this building were located the offices of the Chapman Talent Agency, run by Ed Chapman (Nathan Lane) and his brother, Michael (Michael J. Fox), who was better known (and more successful) when he was the child star Mikey, in *Life With Mikey*.

Walk north a few feet until you reach the gentleman's club called Lace, which is located at 725 Seventh Avenue.

14. Lace. 725 Seventh Avenue (between 48th and 49th Streets). In the days when fear gripped the city, the spot now occupied by this gentleman's club was the site of another one known as Metropole A Go-Go, where much of the action in *Fear City* took place. Inside, the dancers may have been exploited, but they were safe. Outside, in alleys, back streets and other darkened parts of town, someone was attacking the dancers one by one. Luckily, Rossi (Tom Berenger), the ex of Loretta (Melanie Griffith), one of the dancers, was doing his best to bring the assailant to justice and keep the girls safe.

Continue north on Seventh Avenue to 49th Street. Turn left on 49th and walk west until you reach Broadway, a short block away. Turn right on Broadway and walk north one block. From the corner of Broadway and 50th Street, you should get a good glimpse of Paramount Plaza, located on the west side of Broadway, between 50th and 51st Streets.

15. Paramount Plaza. 1633 Broadway. He called a number of times, but never got Jerry Langford (Jerry Lewis) on the phone. Not appreciating such treatment from his idol, zealous fan Rupert Pupkin (Robert De Niro) stopped by to see Jerry, whose studio was in this building, claiming that he was "in the neighborhood." Although that tactic didn't work, when he left the building, he ran into fellow Langford fan Marsha (Sandra Bernhard) and together, in *The King of Comedy*, they began to hatch a plot they thought would satisfy them both.

Continue north on Broadway to 51st Street. Turn left on 51st, cross Broadway, and walk west until you reach the Hotel Washington-Jefferson, at 318 West 51st Street.

16. Hotel Washington-Jefferson. 318 West 51st Street. Ray (Woody Allen) had a brilliant moneymaking scheme: Buy a store, dig from its basement into the bank two doors down, and remove all the cash. But Ray's plan had one major hitch: the store had just been purchased by a woman named Nettie Goldberg. After learning that Nettie lived here, Ray went to make her an offer. But when he arrived, he faced an even big-

ger surprise, finding out that Nettie was none other than Benny (Jon Lovitz), another small-time crook Ray had known in prison. After hearing Ray's plan, Benny agreed to join Ray's gang of *Small Time Crooks*.

Return to Eighth Avenue and make a left. Go north on Eighth one block, to 52nd Street. Turn right on 52nd Street and walk east until you are in front of Floats.

17. Floats. 240 West 52nd Street (between Eighth Avenue and Broadway). Their cross-country tour was a success, but all good things must come to an end. Such was the case for the members of the band Stillwater, one of their most loyal followers, Penny Lane (Kate Hudson) and underage "Rolling Stone" reporter William Miller (Patrick Fugit), all of whom had a celebratory dinner in what was Max's Kansas City, on this site, near the end of *Almost Famous*. At dinner, William informed the members of the band that they were going to be on the cover of "Rolling Stone." It was great news, but they all still had some major obstacles to overcome.

Continue east on 52nd Street and stop across from Roseland, the famed venue of dance.

18. Roseland. 239 West 52nd Street. Not every nightspot has a movie named for it, but this one does. In *Roseland*, a movie that took place almost entirely within this building, people gathered night after night, hoping to find someone to dance with, perhaps someone to love and, at the very least, just a little bit of happiness to help them through their humdrum lives.

Continue walking east until you reach Broadway. Turn left on Broadway and walk north to 54th Street. Make a left on 54th and walk west until you reach another legendary nighttime destination, Studio 54.

19. Studio 54. 254 West 54th Street. They went somewhere else earlier in the evening but quickly learned that the punk scene wasn't for them. And with good reason, for these were the 70s, when disco reigned supreme, and nowhere more so than here, at Studio 54. Newly married, Vinnie (John Leguziamo) and Dionna (Mira Sorvino) came here to be with fellow lovers of the disco beat, but during the *Summer of Sam*, things didn't always work out the way it was hoped. They were selected to join a group that was heading elsewhere, and they ended the evening at Plato's Retreat, a place even more decadent than Studio 54.

Continue west to Eighth Avenue, turn right and walk north one block to 55th Street. Turn right on 55th and walk east. You will almost immediately see Soup Kitchen International on the other side of the street.

20. Soup Kitchen International. 259-A West 55th Street. Immortalized by a classic episode of the television show "Seinfeld," this popular eatery is the real-life location of the "Soup Nazi" depicted on the show. If it's open, feel free to get on

line and enjoy the soup. But have your money ready, order and quickly step to the left, and don't mention Seinfeld. Word has it that the proprietor is not a fan, despite the publicity the show has generated for this storefront business.

Continue east on 55th Street. At the far side of Seventh Avenue, turn right and walk south to 853 Seventh Avenue, between 54th and 55th Street.

21. The Wyoming. 853 Seventh Avenue (between 54th and 55th Streets). Linda (Andie MacDowell) lived in this building, which offered her a brief respite from the shenanigans and schemes of her on-again, off again boyfriend Gary (Andy Garcia), who had his own ideas about how to make an honest buck, in *Just the Ticket.*

Continue south to 54th Street and turn left. Walk east until you reach the Ziegfeld Theatre, halfway between Seventh and Sixth Avenues.

22. Ziegfeld Theatre. 141 West 54th Street. Although Flo Ziegfeld staged his big-budget spectacles in a Times Square theater (see Location 2 of this Walking Tour), the theater that bears his name was the site of a celebrity-packed premiere for the film "The Liquidator," starring Nicole Oliver (Melanie Griffith), in the movie *Celebrity.*

Continue on to Avenue of the Americas and turn right. Walk south four blocks until you are across from Radio City Music Hall, at 50th Street.

23. Radio City Music Hall. 1260 Avenue of the Americas. One of his fondest and most vivid memories of childhood connected to an old radio song was when his Aunt Bee (Dianne Wiest) and her boyfriend took Joe (Seth Green, the son of Dr. Evil in the Austin Powers movies) to Radio City Music Hall. Such an outing was a rare occurrence for Joe and his family, and it happened in *Radio Days.*

Poor Joe. He had to attend a show at Radio City along with everyone else who had a ticket for that evening's performance. Not so for little orphan Annie. Thanks to her extreme great fortune in falling into the lap of the ultra-wealthy Oliver "Daddy" Warbucks (Albert Finney), Annie (Aileen Quinn) was treated to a command performance here, after Daddy Warbucks rented out the place. In *Annie*, she came here with Warbucks and the beautiful Grace (Ann Reinking).

Cross over to Radio City Music Hall and continue east on 50th Street until you are in front of the Rockefeller Center Garage, at 41 West 50th Street.

24. Rockefeller Center Garage. 41 West 50th Street. There was a *Saboteur* on the loose, and Barry Kane (Robert Cummings) was the primary suspect. He was taken by car into this garage, and then upstairs to the offices of American Newsreel, Inc. But then the shooting started and Barry fled, free to find the real criminal (Norman Lloyd) before it was too late.

Continue east on 50th Street until you emerge at the plaza of Rockefeller Center. Turn to the left. The AOL Time Warner Building is one block to the north, at 75 Rockefeller Plaza.

25. AOL Time Warner Building. 75 Rockefeller Plaza. He was doing okay, but with the expenses piling up, Tommy (Gregory Peck) knew that he had to do better. He came here for a job interview with the United Broadcasting Corporation and got the job, but in *The Man in the Gray Flannel Suit*, Tommy learned that a part of his past was about to catch up to him.

Turn around and find a safe vantage point to view the skating rink at Rockefeller Center.

26. Rockefeller Center Skating Rink. A popular location that finds its way into movies time and again, the rink is at its most magical during the cold winter months, when skaters glide gracefully across the slick, glistening surface. When her brother Adam (Cliff Robertson) told her he was going ice-skating with his "virtuous" friend Mona, Eileen (Jane Fonda) came here to find him, never imagining that, as intended by Adam, ice-skating was a euphemism. On a *Sunday in New York*, Eileen met a stranger on a bus who gallantly offered to help her find her brother. They came here, but of course, couldn't find him. So Eileen and the stranger, Mike (Rod Taylor), decided to get acquainted at a table overlooking the skating rink.

His uncle wanted him to dump his girlfriend Elizabeth (Margaux Hemingway), but Alby Sherman (Elliott Gould) was hoping to borrow money from his uncle to open a Manhattan restaurant without giving in to that one demand. During a night on the town, in *Over the Brooklyn Bridge*, Alby and Elizabeth came here to skate.

Clearly a popular place for a date, the skating rink is also where Ann (Liv Ullman) and Peter (Edward Albert) came to discuss their relationship. In *40 Carats*, it had started in an idyllic overseas setting and Ann thought it should end there, because she was so much older than Peter. But when they met up again in New York, Peter wanted things to continue and even confessed his love for her. Ann denied having the same feelings for him, but they both knew she was lying.

A few years later, another May-December romance seemed to be blossoming on the ice. In *Autumn in New York*, Will Keane (Richard Gere) had almost put aside his bachelor ways to devote himself to Charlotte (Winona Ryder), his much younger girlfriend. As the weather turned colder and autumn inched toward winter, Will walked alongside as Charlotte skated, but when she collapsed on the ice, they knew their autumn was almost over.

Walk around the skating rink and exit Rockefeller Plaza toward Fifth Avenue. Turn back and get a good look at the tallest building around, on the far side of the skating rink.

27. 30 Rockefeller Plaza. The Rainbow Room. It is no longer the elite venue it was then, but in 1940, it was the place to go, and in *The Curse of the Jade Scorpion*, this is where George Bond (Wallace Shawn) was taken to celebrate his 50th birthday. During dinner, George and his colleagues from the North Coast Fidelity and Casualty Insurance Company were entertained by hypnotist Voltan Polgar (David Ogden Stiers), but after two of the colleagues, insurance investigator C.W. Briggs (Woody Allen) and efficiency expert Betty Ann Fitzgerald (Helen Hunt) were hypnotized, the hypnotist's criminal scheme was set in motion.

Turn back to Fifth Avenue and walk to the curb.

28. Fifth Avenue, in front of Rockefeller Plaza. After an acting audition, Marjorie (Natalie Wood) stepped from the curb into a car driven by David (Martin Balsam). He wasn't Noel Airman (Gene Kelly), on whom Marjorie had once had a crush, but a lot of time had passed since then. At least for a while, not being Noel was probably a good thing, in *Marjorie Morningstar*.

Look at Sak's Fifth Avenue, across the street.

29. Sak's Fifth Avenue. 611 Fifth Avenue. It was the night before Christmas, and neither Frank (Robert De Niro) nor Molly (Meryl Streep) had finished their holiday shopping.

Tour 8

Along with thousands of others who waited until the last minute, Frank and Molly came here to shop. They didn't know each other at the time and their paths didn't cross, but there were a few near misses and both should have known that, in *Falling in Love*, it would only be a matter of time.

Professor Alcott (Greg Kinnear) was bringing Dora (Mena Suvari) to meet his parents, but first, he insisted on buying her some new clothes. While shopping at this store, Dora finally began to realize that Alcott didn't like her for who she was, but rather, for what he wanted her to be. Once he lost Dora, Alcott became the *Loser*.

Turn left and walk north until you are across from St. Patrick's Cathedral, across Fifth.

30. Fifth Avenue, in front of St. Patrick's Cathedral. Easter is traditionally the day when people put on their very best clothes, adorn themselves with the most lavish of Easter bonnets, and saunter along with their loved ones, friends and strangers, all marching in The Parade. And that's what Don Hewes (Fred Astaire) and Hannah Brown (Judy Garland) did, along Fifth Avenue in front of this Cathedral, in *Easter Parade*.

Before continuing north, turn around and admire the statue of Atlas, behind you, in front of 630 Fifth Avenue, between 50th and 51st Streets.

31. Statue of Atlas. 630 Fifth Avenue (between 50th and 51st Streets). Most people stand below this statue and can't help but admire Atlas, his build and his strength. But Hercules (Arnold Schwarzenegger) was not like most people. In *Hercules in New York*, Hercules noted that this statue was not a very good likeness of Atlas, and Hercules was in a position to know.

Now continue north on Fifth Avenue and turn left on 52nd Street. Walk west until you are across from the "21" Club.

32. "21" Club. 21 West 52nd Street. They were old beyond their years, although not necessarily any wiser for it. In *Metropolitan*, two confirmed city dwellers from families of means, Serena (Elizabeth Thompson) and Tommy (Edward Clements), had drinks here, a place more accustomed to serving those of an earlier generation. Among other things, they discussed how Tommy had saved every letter that Serena had sent him.

You have now reached the end of **Walking Tour 8: The Broadway Beat**.

Walking Tour 9

Gramercy Garden Grand

Uptown
West Side
East Side
Downtown

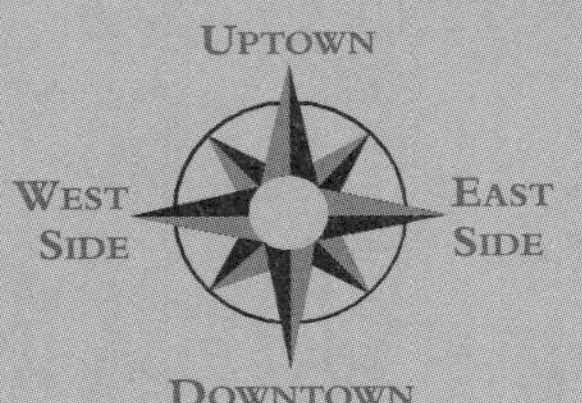

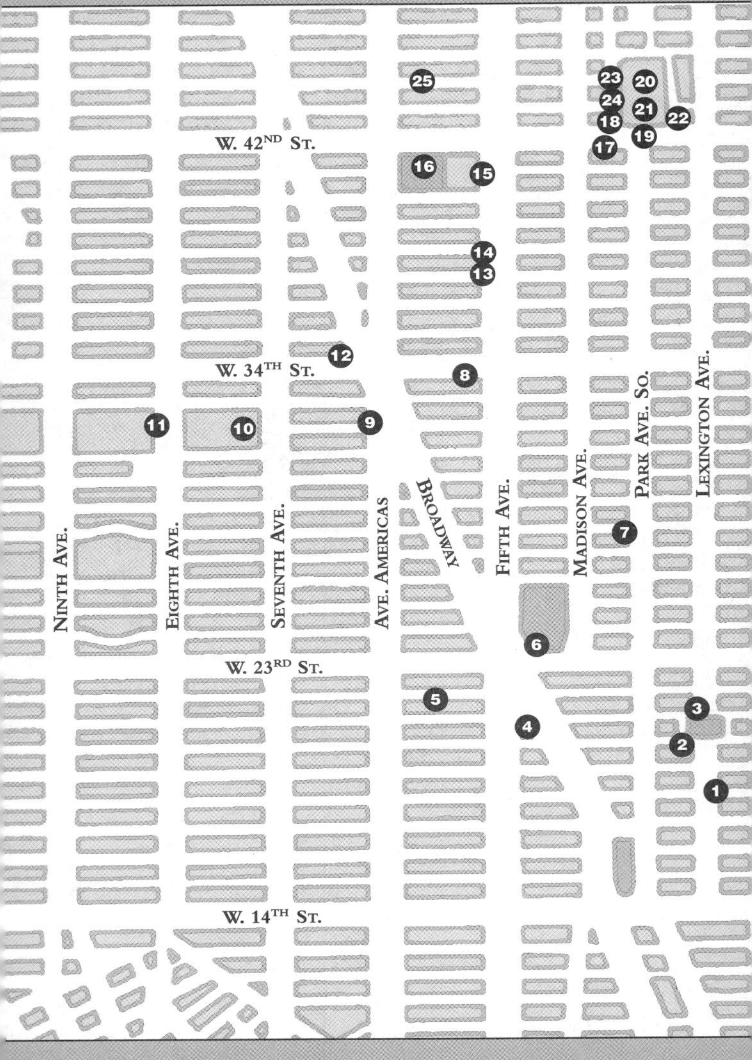
W. 42ND St.
W. 34TH St.
W. 23RD St.
W. 14TH St.
Ninth Ave.
Eighth Ave.
Seventh Ave.
Ave. Americas
Broadway
Fifth Ave.
Madison Ave.
Park Ave. So.
Lexington Ave.
1
2
3
4
5
6
7
8
9
10
11
12
13
14
15
16
17
18
19
20
21
22
23
24
25

Walking Tour 9

Gramercy Garden Grand

As the name so cleverly suggests, **Walking Tour 9: Gramercy Garden Grand** will cover three of the most well known venues in New York City. Beginning in the upscale and exclusive Gramercy Park area, it winds its way to Madison Square Garden, one of the most famous sports and entertainment arenas in the world, and eventually finds its way to Grand Central Station, a legendary, majestic and immensely photogenic transportation hub. Along the way, you will discover some great locations from a diverse sampling of movies.

Walking Tour 9: Gramercy Garden Grand begins near Union Square Park, which is bordered by 14th and 17th Streets on the south and north, respectively, Broadway on the west and Park Avenue South on the east. The first location of this walking tour is slightly east of the park, so the closer you get to the park, the better, unless otherwise indicated below. If you choose to take public transportation to Union Square Park, you may use any of the following subway or bus lines (although the following list is by no means exhaustive):

FROM THE NORTH

SUBWAYS

- **4, 5** or **6** southbound to 14th Street/Union Square.
- **Q** or **W** southbound to 14th Street/Union Square.

- **N** or **R** southbound to 14th Street/Union Square.

Buses

- **M1** southbound on Fifth Avenue, then Park Avenue, then Park Avenue South, to 17th Street.
- **M2**, **M3** or **M5** southbound on Fifth Avenue to 17th Street. Walk east on 17th to Park Avenue South.
- **M6** or **M7** southbound on Seventh Avenue, then Broadway, to 17th Street.
- **M101, M102** or **M103** southbound on Lexington Avenue, then Third Avenue, to 18th Street. Walk west on 18th to Irving Place.

FROM THE SOUTH

Subways

- **4, 5** or **6** northbound to 14th Street/Union Square.
- **Q** or **W** northbound to 14th Street/Union Square.
- **N** or **R** northbound to 14th Street/Union Square.

Buses

- **M103** northbound on Bowery, then Third Avenue, to 18th Street. Walk west on 18th to Irving Place.

FROM THE EAST

Subways

- **L** (14th Street Shuttle) westbound to Union Square.

Buses

- **M14** westbound on 14th Street, to Union Square.

FROM THE WEST

SUBWAYS

- **L** (14th Street Shuttle) eastbound to Union Square.

BUSES

- **M14** eastbound on 14th Street to Union Square.

If the above directions already brought you to Irving Place and 18th, you are right where you should be. If not, assuming you are somewhere near Union Square Park, walk north to 18th Street and then east to Irving Place (one block east of the park). You should see Pete's Tavern on the northeast corner of Irving Place and 18th.

1. Pete's Tavern. 129 East 18th Street (at Irving Place). One of the oldest pubs in Manhattan, dating back to when Abraham Lincoln was president, Pete's is where Jerry Ryan (Robert Mitchum) stopped in to have a drink in *Two For*

the Seesaw, after spending a long day walking around the city. He had come to New York to practice law after his marriage had fallen apart, but even a drink did little to ease his pain.

Walk north on Irving Place. At 20th Street (Gramercy Park South), turn left and walk the short distance until you reach the National Arts Club, at 15 Gramercy Park South.

2. National Arts Club. 15 Gramercy Park South. A valuable painting had already been stolen from the Metropolitan Museum of Art, and insurance investigator Catherine Banning (Rene Russo) was on the case. At a fundraiser held here, she introduced herself to billionaire businessman Thomas Crown (Pierce Brosnan) and told him she knew far more about him than he would have expected, including his suspected involvement in the museum theft. All this piqued his interest and their affair was not far off on the horizon, in *The Thomas Crown Affair.*

Walk west from the National Arts Club and turn right at Gramercy Park West. Then make a right on Gramercy Park North (21st Street) and walk the short distance to Lexington Avenue. The Gramercy Park Hotel is on the northwest corner of Lexington and Gramercy Park North.

3. Gramercy Park Hotel. 52 Gramercy Park North. When their 1973 tour ended, members of the band Stillwater, upon arriving in New York, checked in here, in *Almost Famous*.

Turn back west on Gramercy Park North and continue past Park Avenue South one more block until you reach Broadway. Look at the restaurant across Broadway from where you stand.

4. Metronome. 915 Broadway (at 21st Street). It started with an insult and embarrassment, then escalated all the way to murder. After a friendly dinner inside this restaurant turned deadly, John Shaft (Samuel L. Jackson) took up the case and pursued it even after giving up his police shield, in *Shaft*.

Walk north on Broadway to 22nd Street. Turn left on 22nd and walk west until you are halfway between Fifth and Sixth Avenues, where you will reach Lola.

5. Lola. 30 West 22nd Street. In *The Best Man,* after the pre-wedding celebratory dinner that was held here ended, the wedding was still on because the groom had not yet learned about

his fiancée and his best man and their somewhat romantic past, but Julian (Harold Perrineau, Jr.) and Shelby (Melissa De Sousa) had problems of their own to talk about.

Turn back and walk east to Fifth Avenue. Turn left and walk north on Fifth until you reach the south side of 23rd Street. Madison Square Park is before you, slightly to the right.

6. Madison Square Park. Fifth Avenue and 23rd Street. The government was cracking down and the likelihood of putting on a show was diminishing with each passing day. But in *Cradle Will Rock*, the playwright Marc (Hank Azaria) refused to give up. One hectic afternoon, he sat on a bench in this park, imagining the musical he was writing, while police rode by on horseback and hit people with their nightsticks. It was a surreal scene indeed.

Turn right and walk east on 23rd Street, keeping the park on your left. Turn left on Park Avenue South and walk north until you reach the southwest corner of Park and 28th Street.

7. Park Avenue South and 28th Street. Subway entrance on southwest corner. A subway train had been hijacked and the cops raced to get the ransom money before it was too late. In *The Taking of Pelham One, Two, Three*, they took the money and descended this staircase to the subway that was in jeopardy, somewhere down below.

Continue north on Park Avenue South and turn left on 33rd Street. Walk west on 33rd but stop when you reach Madison Avenue. Admire the Empire State Building towering above you, one block to the west.

8. Empire State Building. 350 Fifth Avenue (at 34th Street). As you admire the proud structure before you, make sure that you remain safely on the curb. Terry McKay (Irene Dunne) didn't, and she paid a heavy price for her lapse. Rushing to keep her rendezvous with Michel Marnay (Charles Boyer) on the pre-arranged day (July 1) at the pre-arranged time, Terry was looking up when the car hit her. In *Love Affair*, an increasingly despondent Michel waited on the Observation Deck high atop the building. As the day turned increasingly stormy, Michel wondered aloud if the woman he loved would ever show. And when she didn't, he finally left there alone, not understanding what could possibly have gone wrong.

For Terry, reaching the Observation Deck

would have taken a Herculean effort that day, but for Hercules (Arnold Strong, a.k.a. Arnold Schwarzenegger), such efforts came with the territory. With his new friend Pretzel (Arnold Stang), he came up here to admire the view at the end of *Hercules in New York*. But while Pretzel enjoyed his first visit to this spot, he lost sight of his friend, and when he went to find him, could not. Pretzel didn't know that "Herc" had been summoned back home to Olympus, his New York adventure at an end.

Continue west on 33rd Street one more block. When you reach Sixth Avenue, the Manhattan Mall will be directly before you.

9. Manhattan Mall. 100 West 33rd Street (at Sixth Avenue). Gary (Andy Garcia) came here to pay a surprise visit to his ex-girlfriend, Linda (Andie MacDowell), where she worked in an electronics store inside this mall. But she wasn't interested in talking, having all but given up on their relationship, in *Just the Ticket*. But she agreed to change her mind if Gary convinced a potential customer to buy a giant TV, a customer Linda thought was too cheap to buy even a toaster. A skillful salesman with the gift of gab, Gary got his chance to talk to Linda after all.

Cross Sixth Avenue and continue west one block, to Seventh Avenue. Madison Square Garden will be across Seventh from you.

10. Madison Square Garden. Seventh Avenue and 32nd Street. Eddie (Whoopi Goldberg) was an avid fan of the New York Knicks and came here to watch every home basketball game. During a promotional event sponsored by the team's new owner, Wild Bill Burgess (Frank Langella), Eddie sank a basket during halftime and was made the team's honorary coach for the second half of the game. But after the real coach, John Bailey (Dennis Farina) had her thrown out of the arena, Wild Bill decided to get his revenge and made Eddie the coach on a full-time basis. A

dream come true for any avid sports fan, and one that became a reality for *Eddie*.

The Knicks were again the subject when Jamal Wallace (Rob Brown) convinced recluse William Forrester (Sean Connery) to leave his apartment and celebrate his birthday by attending a basketball game, in *Finding Forrester*. But when they got separated on the way into the garden, William became scared and disoriented, and experienced a vivid reminder of why he had stopped leaving his home. The anxiety attack sent the two of them from the garden without watching the game. A few weeks later, however, Jamal was back here playing in a basketball tournament.

Turn right and walk north to 33rd Street. There's no need to walk the one block to see it, but if you feel so inclined or have to buy stamps, you can head west on 33rd to Eighth Avenue, where the main branch of the United States Post Office is located.

11. Post Office. Main Branch. Eighth Avenue and 33rd Street. He met his wife-to-be in Central Park and honeymooned in Atlantic City, but eventually had to return to his job, here. Chet Keefer (Aldo Ray) took a lot of ribbing from his colleagues for tying the knot, but because he was *The Marrying Kind*, he knew his days as a single man had been numbered, anyway.

Assuming you did not walk to the Post Office, turn right and walk north to 34th Street. If you did, retrace your steps and proceed to Seventh and 34th as well. The venerable Macy's should be directly across 34th Street from you. Turn right and walk east until you reach Broadway. Turn and look at Macy's from your vantage point at Broadway and 34th Street.

12. Macy's. Herald Square. 151 West 34th Street. In *Love With the Proper Stranger*, this is where Angela (Natalie Wood) worked, on the fifth floor, in the pet department. When her father and brothers came to pick her up in their

fruit truck, she was embarrassed but put such feelings aside because, that is what one does with family. Later in the film, Rocky (Steve McQueen), trying to patch things up with her, greeted her out front, banjo in hand, with a sign that said "Better Wed Than Dead." Poor Angela was embarrassed yet again, but she put such feelings aside once again, for that is what one does with one's future spouse.

Continue east on 34th Street to Fifth Avenue. Make a left on Fifth and walk north three blocks until you reach the north side of 37th Street.

13. Fifth Avenue and 37th Street. Northwest corner. He landed his dream date with Sally (Marceline Day) and they boarded a double-decker bus at this corner. But the crowd pushing on to the bus was so great that the aptly named Buster (Buster Keaton) was forced to the upper deck while his date got a seat down below, in *The Cameraman*.

Continue north on Fifth Avenue, half a block until you are in front of Lord & Taylor.

14. Lord & Taylor. 424 Fifth Avenue (between 37th and 38th Streets). Michael Chapman (Michael J. Fox) knew all about being a child star. But with those days behind him, he turned his endeavors to representing other child stars, together with his brother Ed (Nathan Lane). But life with their newest client, Angie (Christina Vidal), was proving to be a few tuna fish sandwiches short of a picnic. In *Life With Mikey*, Angie was picked up for shoplifting here after walking out on her agents, and possibly her career. But in the spirit of the holiday season, the security guards let her go, especially after the commercial she had made was aired on TV.

Continue your northward trek on Fifth Avenue until you reach 40th Street. The New York Public Library should now be in full view on your left.

15. New York Public Library. Fifth Avenue

(between 40th and 42nd Streets). He discovered a piece of microfilm in a wallet he had lifted from the purse of an unsuspecting woman on the subway, and though he lived under the Brooklyn Bridge, down on South Street, Skip McCoy (Richard Widmark) came here to do his research. In *Pickup on South Street*, Skip put the microfilm into a machine in the library to see what he had stumbled onto.

When Skip walked into the building, he may have passed Murray Burns (Jason Robards) who, along with a thousand other clowns, was standing in this neighborhood. But there was one marked difference. As Murray stood, binoculars in hand, beside his nephew Nick (Barry Gordon), he told the boy to watch for the horror he was about to witness: people going to work. Murray may have been a bit of a clown, but he wasn't like the others, like *A Thousand Clowns*.

Keeping the library on your left, walk north to 42nd Street. If you choose, you may turn left on 42nd and walk west until you reach Bryant Park, halfway between Fifth and Sixth Avenues. Whether you take this little detour or not, this is what you will find in the park.

16. Bryant Park. Between Fifth and Sixth Avenues (from 40th Street to 42nd Street). During Fashion Week, enormous tents are erected in Bryant Park and many designers hold their annual fashion shows here, where they introduce their new lines of clothing. Because *Head Over Heels* involved a few models, it should come as no surprise that the models had to take time out from their otherwise chaotic lives to walk the runways here. They were all on the run from a Russian smuggler of illegal diamonds, but because the show must go on, Amanda (Monica Potter) and her model/roommates did their part to assist the designer, Mr.

Alfredo (Stanley DeSantis), in showing his latest fashions.

If you chose to go to Bryant Park, return to Fifth Avenue and 42nd Street. If not, you should be on the same southwest corner of that intersection. In either event, cross Fifth Avenue and head east on 42nd Street until you are in front of 70 East 42nd Street.

17. Barclay-Rex Pipe Shop. 70 East 42nd Street (at Vanderbilt Avenue). He had escaped from the federal marshals who were pursuing him from state to state, and he found himself in New York. Although he was on the lam, Mark Sheridan (Wesley Snipes) was intent on clearing his name. But doing so would not be easy. His first stop was in here, where his reception was less than cordial. Thereafter, he knew he would be on his own in his race with Deputy Sam Gerard (Tommy Lee Jones) and the rest of the *U.S. Marshals*.

From where you are standing, look across 42nd Street to the corner of Grand Central Station, at Vanderbilt Avenue.

18. 42nd Street and Vanderbilt Avenue. Northeast corner. Sent to the Earth's surface to bring his trouble-making brothers back down to hell, Satan's childlike son Nicky (Adam Sandler) exited Grand Central Station and encountered a blind preacher (Quentin Tarentino) on this corner, in *Little Nicky*. Although the man was blind, or maybe because of that fact, he could sense that Nicky's appearance in this world could only mean trouble.

Cross 42nd Street and enter Grand Central Station. Work your way down the ramp and turn right into the cavernous central room of the palatial structure. Make your way to the information booth in the middle of the room. Through cinematic history, Grand Central has seen it all and from this spot, you should be able to see it all, too.

19. Grand Central Station. His movie career had all but faded, and former screen star Tony Hunter (Fred Astaire) decided to give Broadway a chance. Disembarking from a train into Grand Central, the soon-to-be Broadway star answered a few questions, but as he walked away, realized he was going his way, by himself, and he so sang, in *The Band Wagon*.

Tony nonchalantly eased his way into the station. Luckily, he hadn't been on the subway train that pulled into Grand Central after two young men with nothing better to do terrorized innocent people on board during a long, harrowing ride. The two bad seeds who caused *The Incident* were Joe (Tony Musante) and Artie (Martin Sheen) and the mostly sheep-like passengers included Ed McMahon (who had taken the subway late at night to save a couple of bucks, something his wife would not let him forget during the entire ride), Jack Gilford, Thelma Ritter, Donna Mills, Brock Peters and Ruby Dee. Luckily for all of them, a passenger,

Private First Class Felix (Beau Bridges), with his arm in a cast, finally stood up and beat the two bullies to a pulp.

The passengers on that train could have used the intervention of Superman. Sadly, he hadn't been around to come to the rescue, but years later, his arch nemesis Lex Luthor (Gene Hackman) maintained an underground lair, down under the tracks below Grand Central Station. *In Superman*, Luthor's bumbling associate Otis (Ned Beatty) strolled through the station and entered the tracks to get to the lair, oblivious to the fact that he was being followed by the police.

And after their train pulled into the station, Frank (Robert De Niro) and Molly (Meryl Streep) made their way to adjacent pay phones, never dreaming that their lives would soon overlap in a much bigger way, in *Falling in Love*. Soon they were spending a good deal of time together and waiting for each other in Grand Central Station before boarding their train.

Of course, all of the above occurred before life as we know it changed, and humans battled apes everywhere, including under this building, in *Beneath the Planet of the Apes*.

While you are standing near the information booth, keep an eye out for a beautiful young woman, sleeping soundly with her back up against the booth.

20. Grand Central Station. Information Booth. After she missed her train, she must have felt like a loser. But Dora (Mena Suvari) made the best of the situation. She called home from a pay phone and told her family that she was staying at her college dorm. With nowhere else to turn, she plopped down in the deserted room you are now in and spent the night trying to sleep, her back against the very information booth in front of which you are now standing. Oddly enough, she was not the one who was considered the *Loser*.

Without taking a step, you should be able to see the ticket booths lining the southern wall of the room. Look for Ticket Window 15.

21. Grand Central Station. Ticket Window 15. On the run for a murder he didn't commit, Roger Thornhill (Cary Grant) phoned his mother, telling her he was leaving town on a train. His destination? It wasn't clear, but it was obvious that the direction he would be heading was *North By Northwest*. After the phone call, he tried to buy a ticket at Window 15. But knowing he had been spotted, Roger immediately boarded a train and, thanks to the kindheartedness of Eve Kendall (Eva Marie Saint), he was able to elude the police until the train pulled out of the station. Only later would he learn why Eve was so eager to help.

There are lockers somewhere in Grand Central, where people can store their belongings, but there's no need to go looking for them. I'll tell you what you would find, if you had.

22. Grand Central Station. Lockers. The phone rang late at night and a soothing yet firm voice instructed C.W. Briggs (Woody Allen) to steal some jewels from the mansion of one of his firm's clients. Stealing was not something that Briggsy, an insurance investigator for the North Coast Fidelity and Casualty Company would typically do, but because the man with the soothing voice (David Ogden Stiers) had hypnotized him, Briggsy was under the *The Curse of the Jade Scorpion* and, therefore, helpless to resist. As per the man's instructions, Briggsy swiped the jewels and placed them in a locker here.

From your vantage point, turn and face the escalators that lead north out of Grand Central Station. Now turn left and walk toward the steps leading up to Vanderbilt Avenue. Climb these steps and exit the building. There is a taxi line just off Vanderbilt Avenue.

23. Vanderbilt Avenue Taxi Line. Outside Grand Central Station. There are times in New York when it is difficult to get a taxi: New Year's Eve, during rainstorms, during strikes. But in the New York of *The Bone Collector*, getting the taxi wasn't the hard part—it was getting a taxi that wasn't being driven by the vicious serial killer who was carrying out a grisly series of murders. An old man and a little girl got into the killer's taxi after waiting on this line, and thought they had gotten lucky when the cops flagged them down. But their luck quickly faded, when the driver shot one cop and sped away with his pair of soon-to-be victims.

Cross Vanderbilt Avenue at the nearest intersection, being careful to avoid traffic. Stop briefly when you get to the west side of Vanderbilt (the side away from Grand Central Station).

24. Vanderbilt Avenue, near 43rd Street (across from Grand Central Station). She liked to spend every *Sunday in New York*. Little did she know that on one such day she would meet the man of her dreams. Just off the train, Eileen (Jane Fonda) avoided the taxi line you just left and hailed a taxi on this spot. She was heading to her brother's apartment. Interestingly enough, Eileen gave the cabdriver the address of "120 East 65th Street" but when she got out of the cab, she entered a building that had "184" on the awning.

Tour 9

Walk up Vanderbilt to 44th Street (unless you are already there) and turn left on 44th. Walk west, past Fifth Avenue until you reach the Algonquin Hotel (halfway to Sixth Avenue).

25. Algonquin Hotel. 59 West 44th Street. Still hot on the trail, not-quite super sleuths Charlie (John Ritter) and Arthur (Blaine Novak) followed the lovely subject of their surveillance, Dolores (Dorothy Stratten) here, and

waited to see whom she was meeting. But in *They All Laughed*, the sleuths were impatient, and decided to take things into their own hands, by talking to Dolores.

If the sleuths had been better at their jobs, they may have noticed writer Liz Hamilton (Jacqueline Bisset), who stayed here on her trips to New York. Liz met her agent, Jules Levi (Steven Hill) in the lobby bar and gave him a new manuscript, but it wasn't hers. It was a novel that had been written by her good friend Merry (Candice Bergen), who, as a result, would soon go on to be *Rich and Famous* herself.

You have now reached the end of **Walking Tour 9: Gramercy Garden Grand**.

45 Fifth Avenue

Walking Tour 10

Greenwich Village

UPTOWN
WEST SIDE
EAST SIDE
DOWNTOWN

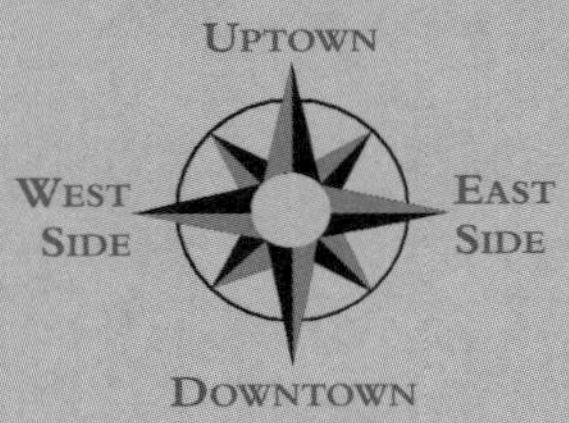

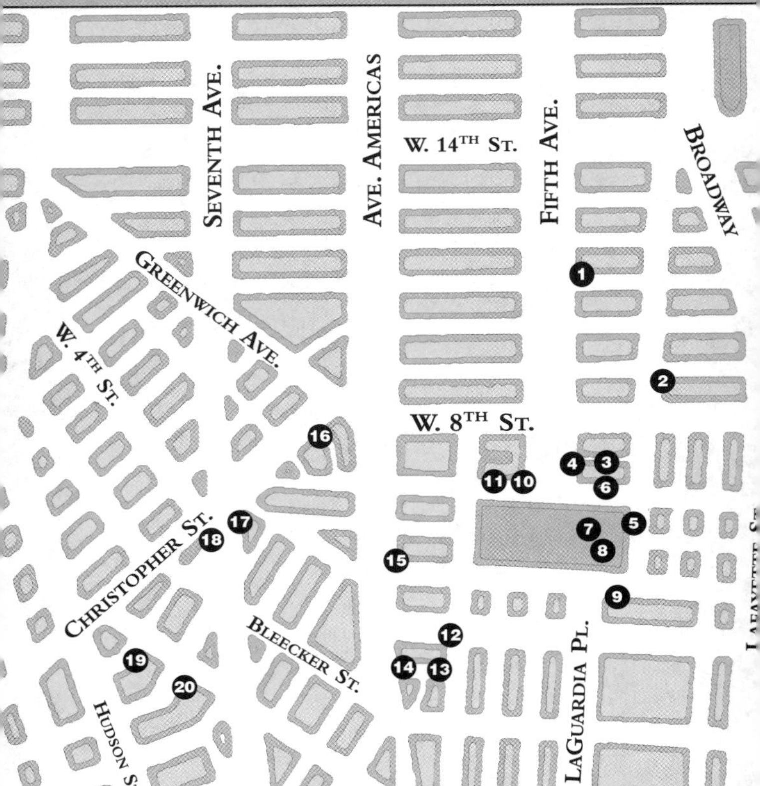

SEVENTH AVE.
AVE. AMERICAS
W. 14TH ST.
FIFTH AVE.
BROADWAY
GREENWICH AVE.
W. 4TH ST.
W. 8TH ST.
CHRISTOPHER ST.
BLEECKER ST.
LAGUARDIA PL.
HUDSON ST.
HOUSTON ST.
1
2
3
4
5
6
7
8
9
10
11
12
13
14
15
16
17
18
19
20
21

Walking Tour 10

Greenwich Village

Long considered the home of New York's funkiest and most bohemian life styles, Greenwich Village is rich with winding streets, beautiful brownstones and endless outdoor cafes that can satisfy the most diverse cross-section of tastes from anywhere in the world.

Walking Tour 10: Greenwich Village begins on 11th Street and Fifth Avenue. If you choose to get to the starting point by public transportation, you may use any of the following subway or bus lines (although the following list is by no means exhaustive):

FROM THE NORTH

SUBWAYS

- **4, 5** or **6** southbound to 14th Street/Union Square.
- **N** or **R** southbound to 14th Street/Union Square.
- **Q** or **W** southbound to 14th Street/Union Square.

BUSES

- **M1** southbound on Fifth Avenue, then Park Avenue, then Park Avenue South, to 11th Street.
- **M2, M3** or **M5** southbound on Fifth Avenue to 11th Street.
- **M6** southbound on Seventh Avenue, then Broadway, to 14th Street. Walk west on 14th to Fifth Avenue.

- **M7** southbound on Seventh Avenue, then Broadway, to 14th Street, then westbound on 14th to Fifth Avenue.

FROM THE SOUTH

SUBWAYS

- **4, 5** or **6** northbound to 14th Street/Union Square.
- **N** or **R** northbound to 14th Street/Union Square.
- **Q** or **W** northbound to 14th Street/Union Square.

BUSES

- **M6** northbound on Avenue of the Americas to 11th Street.

FROM THE EAST

SUBWAYS

- **L** (14th Street Shuttle) westbound to Union Square.

BUSES

- **M14** westbound on 14th Street to Union Square.

FROM THE WEST

SUBWAYS

- **L** (14th Street Shuttle) eastbound to Union Square.

BUSES

- **M14** eastbound on 14th Street to Union Square.

From wherever public transportation has taken you, head south to 11th Street. If you are on Fifth Avenue, stay there. If you are east of Fifth, walk west and if you are on Avenue of the Americas, head east, in both cases, until you reach Fifth. 43 Fifth Avenue is on the northeast corner.

1. 43 Fifth Avenue (Northeast corner of Fifth and 11th Street). He lived in this building and did his best to teach Frenchy (Tracey Ullman) how to fit into high society. His name was David (Hugh Grant), but he wasn't all he claimed to be. In fact, if Frenchy and her husband, Ray (Woody Allen) were *Small Time Crooks*, than David was a big time crook.

Continue south on Fifth Avenue and make a left on 10th Street. Walk east on 10th, turn right on University Place and head south one block, to 9th Street. The Knickerbocker Bar & Grill should be across University Place, on the southeast corner of the intersection.

2. Knickerbocker Bar & Grill. 33 University Place (at 9th Street). From high society scam artist to mobster wannabe, Hugh Grant knows this part of town pretty well. He was doing his best to impress and fit in with Frank (James Caan), his future father-in-law. Walking the walk and talking the talk (although his attempts at "fuhgeddaboutit" left a lot to be desired), Michael (Hugh Grant) came here for a "sit down" with a couple of tough characters. But in *Mickey Blue Eyes*, something always seemed to be going wrong. When Michael saw his auction house boss in the restaurant, and his cover was about to be blown, he had no choice but to scream at the man and forcibly push him outdoors. It almost seemed as if Michael had wandered onto the set of HBO's "The Sopranos," judging by the number of that show's cast members in the movie.

Continue south on University until you are half a block south of 8th Street. On your right should be a gated entrance to the Washington Mews. Assuming the gate is open, walk into the short, picturesque street and stop in front of number 14, on the left side of the street.

Tour 10

3. 14 Washington Mews. He had been given a glimpse of how his life would have turned out, had he married his college sweetheart. Realizing that having a loving wife and kids would have made him happier than all the wealth that his career brought him, Jack Campbell (Nicolas Cage) decided to find his old flame and see if his life could still take the correct turn. Tracking down Kate (Tea Leoni) to her office, which was located in this building, Jack showed up as she was about to move and did his best to make her his again, and to make himself *The Family Man*.

Exit the Mews through the same gate. Before you go anywhere, imagine that you are an orphan, you have just escaped from the orphanage and you are looking for one of your own.

4. Fifth Avenue. Other side of Washington Mews. That is what the orphan girls did in *Annie*, when they snuck out of Miss Hannigan's Home for Girls and went looking for Annie (Aileen Quinn), who was at Daddy Warbuck's mansion, way up Fifth Avenue in another part of New York City, seemingly another part of the world to them. Their journey to find their friend began near One Fifth Avenue, which is very close to here.

Turn right onto University Place. Head south and walk the short block until you reach Washington Square North. Before you turn, note the large building south and to your left, on the east side of Washington Square Park.

5. 100 Washington Square East (between Waverly and Washington Place). Frank Serpico (Al Pacino) was a cop, but still took classes to better himself. And he still found time for a social life. After class, he waited outside this building for Laurie (Barbara Eda-Young), then

gave her a ride on his motorcycle. It wasn't long before she and *Serpico* were an item.

Turn right on Washington Square North and stop in front of number 7.

6. 7 Washington Square North. Virgil (Val Kilmer) had been given the gift of sight, thanks to the devotion and urging of Amy (Mira Sorvino), but his sight, in *At First Sight*, was fleeting. Eventually reverting to blindness, Virgil still considered himself luckier than most, and decided to do what he could to help others in need. Under the tutelage of Dr. Phil Webster (Nathan Lane), Virgil worked as a social worker in this building.

Continue heading west on Washington Square North. When you reach Fifth Avenue, turn and admire the Washington Square Arch.

7. Washington Square Park. Arch. Fifth Avenue Entrance. It was back in the days before the park was closed to vehicular traffic and cars could actually flow through what is now open only to pedestrians. His name was Harold Swift, his nickname was *Speedy* and his goal was to save the last horse-drawn trolley in New York from extinction. Speedy (Harold Lloyd) drove the trolley down Fifth Avenue and under the Arch, doing his best to stay one step ahead of the stereotypical bad guys, who were in hot pursuit.

You may cross and enter the park if you wish, but are under no obligation to do so. From where you are now standing, you should get a good view of the Performance Pit, a few yards south of the Arch.

8. Washington Square Park. Performance Pit. The Performance Pit is a place where jugglers, mimes, musicians and other types of street entertainers can strut their stuff, with passersby stopping to watch and enjoy. In *Three of Hearts*, such passersby were treated to a different kind of spectacle. After her girlfriend Ellen (Sherilyn Fenn) broke up with her, Connie (Kelly Lynch) was so distraught that she stood up and screamed aloud to the world what had just occurred. Ellen had hoped to avoid just such a scene and it wasn't what those nearby were expecting to see, but

it just went to prove that anything can happen in New York and often does.

Not all scenes in and around the Performance Pit are verbal, and not all events are entertaining.

In the stark film *Kids*, which depicted life among a reckless group of poorly-supervised New York City kids, this area was a popular hangout for the gang that was the focus of the movie and in one particularly chilling scene, the kids beat a man within an inch of his life after only the slightest provocation, while onlookers did their best to pretend not to see.

Through the Arch, you can see the red brick building on the south side of the park.

9. Elmer Holmes Bobst Library. 70 Washington Square South. One of the mainstays of the prestigious New York University, this library is a good place to study. And study is what Kathleen Conklin (Lili Taylor) did in *The Addiction*. For one of her courses on human suffering, she spent many nights researching the subject, until she became a vampire and added to the suffering by killing people. Hey, I didn't write the script, I'm just telling you where it was filmed.

If you entered the park, return to Washington Square North and turn left. If you did not, turn right and continue west until you pass Fifth Avenue. Stop about halfway down the block and admire the row of exquisite houses lining the north side of Washington Square Park.

10. Washington Square North (between Fifth Avenue and Washington Square West). New York University now owns many of these buildings, but that wasn't always the case. Closer to the turn of the 20th century, each building housed people of wealth who enjoyed whatever perks could be had in the New York City of that time. Among them was the Sloper family, who lived in one of these buildings. The Slopers consisted of Dr. Austin Sloper (Sir Ralph Richardson), his exceedingly plain daughter, Catherine

(Olivia deHavilland) and Catherine's Aunt Lavinia (Miriam Hopkins). Catherine would inherit a great deal of money some day, and her father was intent on keeping away all unscrupulous suitors, including Morris Townsend (Montgomery Clift), who were more interested in Catherine's status as *The Heiress* of Dr. Sloper than in her as a person and potential wife. *The Heiress* was based on the novel *Washington Square* by Henry James and was remade under that title.

If you are not right in front of it, find 21 Washington Square North, which is on this block.

11. 21 Washington Square North (between Fifth Avenue and Washington Square West). The Sloper family was once again brought to life, as was their life on *Washington Square*, with the same strict yet well-meaning Dr. Sloper (Albert Finney), the same plain Jane of a mark for unscrupulous suitors, Catherine (Jennifer Jason Leigh), the same kindly old Aunt Lavinia (Maggie Smith) and the leader of the pack of heartless cads, Morris Townsend (Ben Chaplin). As in most remakes, the story remained the same and Catherine was again destined to live a long, lonely life.

Continue to the end of the block, which is Washington Square West. Turn left and cross Washington Park North. Walk south, keeping Washington Square Park on your left. You will find that this street will soon become MacDougal Street. Leaving the park behind, continue south. At West 3rd Street, cross to the west side of MacDougal, then resume your southward travel until you reach Caffe Reggio, at 119 MacDougal.

12. Caffe Reggio. 119 MacDougal Street. It was a tough day for John Shaft (Richard Roundtree) and it was going to get tougher.

While sitting in this café sipping his espresso, a man came in and told him they had to go see a lady. But for *Shaft*, nothing was ever easy. A few minutes later, guns were blazing and Shaft got hit.

Sometime after Shaft vacated his table near the back of the café, it was occupied by Larry (Lenny Baker), his girlfriend Sarah (Ellen Greene), Robert (Christopher Walken) and the rest of their gang, who made it a frequent stop, in *Next Stop, Greenwich Village*.

Continue south a few steps until you reach the corner of MacDougal and Minetta Lane. The popular Minetta Tavern should be directly across Minetta Lane from you.

Tour 10

13. Minetta Tavern. 113 MacDougal Street. Although the name was different, called "The La Trattoria," this was the restaurant/bar owned by Frank (James Caan) in *Mickey Blue Eyes*. And although it was a far cry from what he was used to in his world of auction houses and fine pieces of

art, future son-in-law Michael (Hugh Grant) did his best to fit in as one of the gang. Literally.

Jonathan Elliot (Jonathan Silverman) and his

friends also frequented this establishment in the television show, "The Single Guy."

Turn to the right and walk a short distance west on Minetta Lane, keeping Minetta Tavern on your left.

14. Minetta Lane (West of MacDougal Street and next to Minetta Tavern). Adam Sandler has cornered the market on this little stretch of Manhattan. At a loss for how to entertain young Julian (Cole and Dylan Sprouse), with whose care he had been saddled, Sonny (Adam Sandler) finally hit on a sure-fire plan: While Julian looked on in delight, Sonny ran into a moving car on this street and pretended to get hit. In *Big Daddy*, Sonny fell to the ground as Julian broke into laughter.

Tour 10

He had lost his magic flask (the one in which he was to capture his errant satanic brothers), in *Little Nicky*, but thanks to the intervention of Valerie (Patricia Arquette), flask and owner were together once again. Soon afterwards, Nicky (Adam Sandler) and Valerie walked down this street, eating their ice cream cones and getting to know one another.

Continue west on Minetta Lane until you emerge onto Sixth Avenue. Turn right and walk north the short distance until you reach the basketball courts on the east side of the street.

15. Basketball Courts. Sixth Avenue, near West 4th Street. While riding around in a stretch limo, basketball superstar Stacy Patton (Malik Sealy) noticed a pick-up game on these courts, and decided to get in on the action. Because his new coach, Eddie Franklin (Whoopi Goldberg), had given him limited playing time for the Knicks, Patton got some practice by playing one-on-one here, until his mother came by to break up the game, in *Eddie*.

Continue north on Sixth Avenue to Waverly Place. Make a left on Waverly and then a quick right on Gay Street. Walk north on Gay Street until you are in front of number 13.

16. 13 Gay Street. In the movie, the building looked much different, which makes it quite unlikely that the movie was actually filmed here, but the address is unmistakable. In *A Night to Remember*, 13 Gay Street is the building where the Troys (Loretta Young and Brian Aherne) came to live, only to happen upon a murder plot.

Return to Waverly and make a right. Follow the turn of Waverly until you emerge at Seventh Avenue South. Look for the subway entrance at Seventh Avenue South and West 4th.

17. Seventh Avenue South and West 4th Street. Subway Stairs. He started out in Brooklyn but it was *Next Stop, Greenwich Village*.

Suitcases in hand, Larry (Lenny Baker) emerged from the subway, up these stairs, and crossed Seventh Avenue South, passing by Village Cigars, directly across the street. For Larry, he was starting a new life in his new home.

Keep your eyes focused on Village Cigars, across Seventh Avenue South.

18. Village Cigars. 110 Seventh Avenue South. Later that night, or sometime soon after, Larry may have seen actress Alice Detroit (Dyan Cannon) standing on the corner, waiting for her late night rendezvous with playwright Ivan Travalian (Al Pacino), in *Author! Author!* Alice was going to star in Ivan's play, but decided that they might be able to share more than just a professional relationship. Ivan apparently agreed, for when he received Alice's call, giving him only a few minutes to meet her on this corner, he dropped everything and ran.

Cross Seventh Avenue South until you are in front of Village Cigars. Turn left and head south on Seventh Avenue South, then make a quick right on Grove Street. Continue on Grove until you reach Bedford Street. Cross Bedford and find 16 Grove, which should be the second door on your left.

19. 16 Grove Street. Although her school was way up on the Upper East Side of Manhattan (see **Walking Tour 7**, Location 20) and her world was wherever concert pianist Henry Orient (Peter Sellers) happened to be at any given moment in time, this house is where Valerie Boyd (Tippy Walker) lived with parents Isabel (Angela Lansbury) and Frank (Tom Bosley), who were almost never home and, when they were, were not much in the way of parents, in *The World of Henry Orient*.

Return to Bedford Street and make a right. Walk two short blocks and make a right on Commerce Street. Near the bend in the road, you will find the Cherry Lane Theater on your left.

20. Cherry Lane Theater. 38 Commerce Street. *Godspell* was a movie, a rock opera, an inspirational anthem to a decade in America and an era long-since gone. It also contained scenes filmed all over New York. In one particular scene, the cast from the movie put on a skit, complete with piano music and film footage, inside this theater.

And in *Mo' Better Blues*, this entire street was reconstructed to reflect a jazzier time in our history. The music venue Beneath the Underdog, where trumpeter Bleek Gilliam (Denzel Washington) was one of the featured performers, was located in what is now the Cherry Lane.

Return to Bedford Street and make a right. Stay on Bedford until you reach the far side of Downing Street. Le Gamin Café will be on your right.

21. Le Gamin Café. 27 Bedford Street (just

off Downing Street). Laura (Anne Heche) was engaged, but she wasn't completely ready to give up her single ways. She and best friend Amelia (Catherine Keener) spent a lot of time here, drinking coffee and talking. And before long, Laura's innocent flirtation with a waiter had the potential to lead to something more, when she agreed to go see the man in a play. But the play was a bomb and Laura decided to proceed with her wedding as planned, her conscience almost clear, in *Walking and Talking*.

You have now come to the end of **Walking Tour 10: Greenwich Village**.

Coyote
Ugly Saloon

Walking Tour 11

The Lower East Side

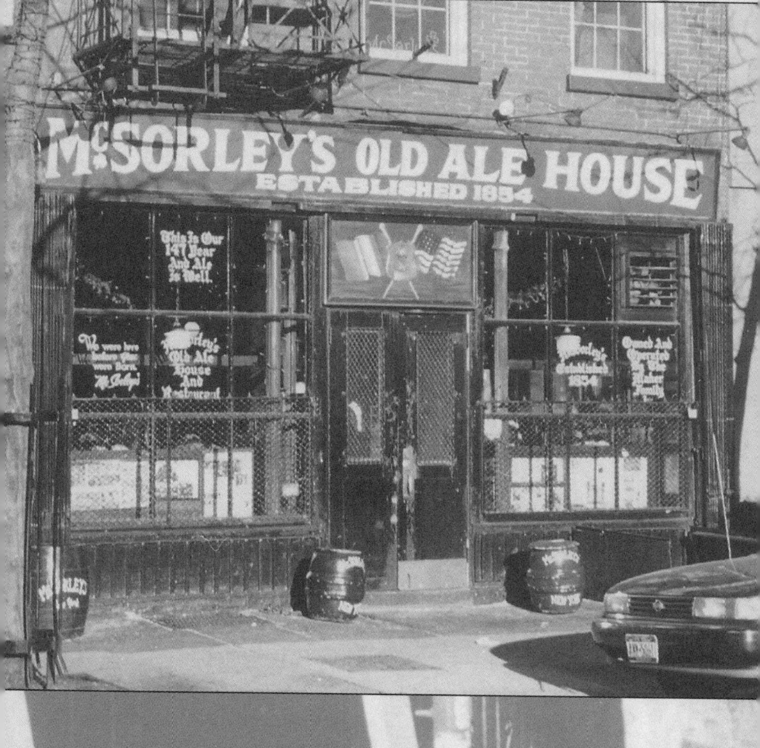

UPTOWN
WEST SIDE
EAST SIDE
DOWNTOWN

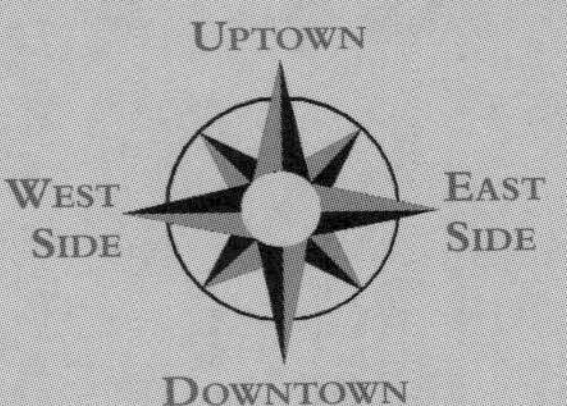

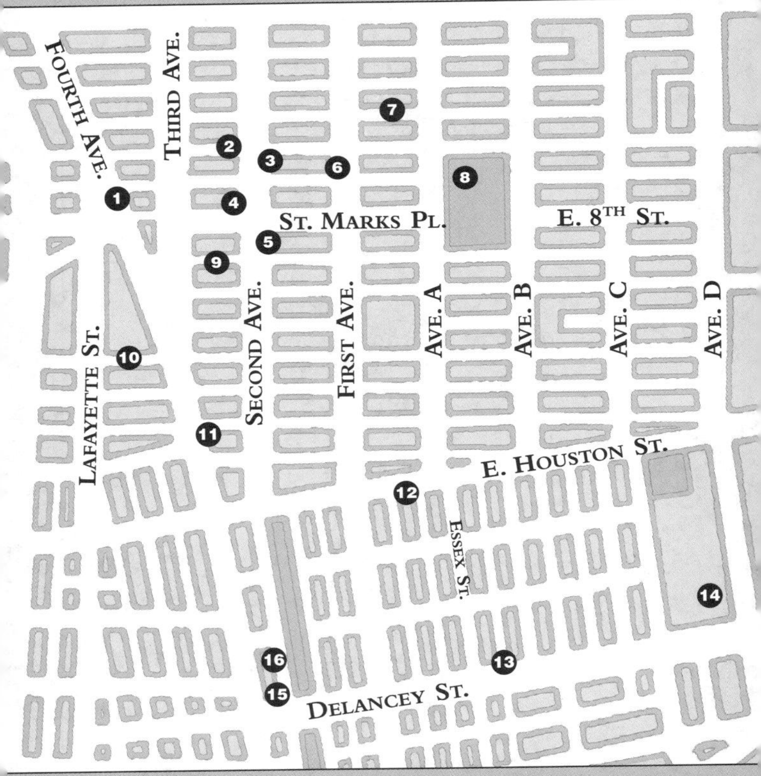
FOURTH AVE.
THIRD AVE.
ST. MARKS PL.
E. 8TH ST.
SECOND AVE.
FIRST AVE.
AVE. A
AVE. B
AVE. C
AVE. D
LAFAYETTE ST.
E. HOUSTON ST.
ESSEX ST.
DELANCEY ST.
1
2
3
4
5
6
7
8
9
10
11
12
13
14
15
16

Walking Tour 11

The Lower East Side

Walking Tour 11: The Lower East Side covers the part of New York that harbors a great confluence of lifestyles, from Bohemian to Grunge, from Heavy Metal to Punk. Known for comparatively cheap eats and bars that cater to every whim imaginable, the Lower East Side has something for everyone.

Walking Tour 11: The Lower East Side begins at the northeast corner of Fourth Avenue and 9th Street, facing a "square" known as Astor Place. If you choose to get to the starting point by public transportation, you may use any of the following subway or bus lines (although the following list is by no means exhaustive):

FROM THE NORTH

Subways

- **4** or **5** southbound to 14th Street/Union Square. Transfer to **6** southbound to Astor Place.
- **6** southbound to Astor Place.
- **N** or **R** southbound to 8th Street. Walk east on 8th to Astor Place.
- **Q** or **W** southbound to 8th Street. Walk east on 8th to Astor Place.

Buses

- **M1** southbound on Fifth Avenue, then Park Avenue, then Park Avenue South, then Broadway, to 9th Street. Walk east on 9th to Fourth Avenue.

- **M2** or **M3** southbound on Fifth Avenue, then eastbound on 8th Street, to Astor Place.
- **M15** southbound on Second Avenue to 9th Street. Walk west on 9th to Fourth Avenue.
- **M101, M102** or **M103** southbound on Lexington Avenue, then Third Avenue, to 9th Street. Walk west on 9th to Fourth Avenue.

FROM THE SOUTH

SUBWAYS

- **6** northbound to Astor Place.
- **N** or **R** northbound to 8th Street. Walk east on 8th to Astor Place.
- **Q** or **W** northbound to 8th Street. Walk east on 8th to Astor Place.

BUSES

- **M103** northbound on Bowery, then Third Avenue, to 9th Street. Walk west on 9th to Fourth Avenue.

FROM THE EAST

SUBWAYS

- **L** (14th Street Shuttle) westbound to Union Square. Walk south on Fourth Avenue to 9th Street.

BUSES

- **M8** westbound on 10th Street, then 9th Street, to Fourth Avenue.
- **M9** or **M14** westbound on 14th Street to Union Square. Walk south on Fourth Avenue to 9th Street.

FROM THE WEST

SUBWAYS

- **L** (14th Street Shuttle) eastbound to Union Square. Walk south on Fourth Avenue to 9th Street.

BUSES

- **M8** eastbound on 10th Street, then 8th Street, to Astor Place.

- **M14** eastbound on 14th Street to Union Square. Walk south on Fourth Avenue to 9th Street.

When you get to Astor Place, find the corner of Fourth Avenue and 9th Street. You should be just north of the ornate subway station entrance on the median.

1. Astor Place Subway Entrance. Finally trying to be more self-assertive, Paul (Jason Biggs) here got up the nerve to ask Dora (Mena Suvari) to go with him to a rock concert. Although he had had a crush on her for a while, he knew he was considered something of a *Loser* and was surprised when she agreed to meet him at the concert at 9:30 p.m., after her job interviews.

Turn from the subway entrance and head north on the east side of Fourth Avenue. Turn right on 10th Street and walk east until you reach Second Avenue. The church known as St. Mark's in the Bowery should be on your left and if you're lucky, some street vendors might be peddling their wares in front of the church, in Abe Lebewohl Park.

2. 10th Street, west of Second Avenue. After his flask had been stolen, one of the devil's children, *Little Nicky* (Adam Sandler), found it being sold by an indignant street vendor (John Witherspoon) and tried to get it back. But he needed help, which he found in the person of Valerie (Patricia Arquette), who happened to come along at the right moment and worked her charm on the vendor. Nicky regained the flask, and found a friend at the same time.

Head south on Second Avenue until you are across from 148 Second Avenue.

3. 148 Second Avenue. Up the few steps in this

nondescript building, *Out-of-Towners* Henry (Steve Martin) and Nancy (Goldie Hawn) went to see if their daughter, who lived here, was home. But she wasn't, so their quest for a place to stay continued.

Continue south on Second and turn right on St. Mark's Place. Walk west the short distance until you are in front of the building just to the right of St. Mark's Deli, which is located at 31 St. Mark's Place.

4. Just to the Right of 31 St. Mark's Place. Five years after their heyday, the Ghostbusters were all off doing different things, as the crisis that had plagued New York dissipated. Ray (Dan Aykroyd) owned a bookstore, called "Ray's Occult Books" on this spot, in *Ghostbusters II.* But after the demons returned, Peter (Bill Murray) and Egon (Harold Ramis) paid a visit to Ray's Occult Books and convinced Ray to put on his ghostbusting uniform once again.

Reverse your direction on St. Mark's, and turn right on Second Avenue. Head south until you are across from the Orpheum Theatre, which is located at 126 Second Avenue.

5. Orpheum Theatre. 126 Second Avenue. He was still trying to balance his love life, which he left behind in Connecticut, with his career ambitions. His play, "Master of My Emotions" was opening here, thanks to the enthusiasm of producer Carl Fisher (Tony Curtis), but playwright Jake (Eric Stoltz) only made things more complicated by getting *Naked in New York* with the play's leading lady, Dana (Kathleen Turner).

Head back north on Second Avenue and make a right on 9th Street. Head east on 9th and then make a left on First Avenue. Coyote Ugly will be on your left, just north of 9th.

6. Coyote Ugly. 153 First Avenue (between 9th and 10th Streets). This is the true location of Coyote Ugly, the focus of the movie of the same name. However, in *Coyote Ugly*, the bar's lo-

cation was moved to the Meat Packing District, in and around 14th Street, Gansevoort Street and Washington Street, many blocks west of here.

Continue north on First Avenue and make a right on 11th Street. Head east on 11th until you are across from the large school, halfway down the block, on the north side of the street.

7. Junior High School 60. 11th Street (between First Avenue and Avenue A). The front of the school is actually on 12th Street, but in *Mickey Blue Eyes*, Michael (Hugh Grant) showed up here where Gina (Jeanne Tripplehorn) was a teacher. With big plans for that night, Michael was anxious to get started.

Continue east on 11th Street and turn right on Avenue A. Head south on Avenue A until you reach 9th Street. At 9th, cross Avenue A and enter Tompkins Square Park. Follow the path as it curves to the right. You will soon come to a large sculpture adorning a water fountain.

8. Sculpture and Water Fountain. Tompkins Square Park. Off 9th Street and Avenue A. He had just arrived in New York and was taking a break from the sketching he was doing in this park. As Finn (Ethan Hawke) stooped to drink from the fountain, he was elated to learn that the tongue licking his face belonged to his lifelong friend Estella (Gwyneth Paltrow), and not a

promiscuous squirrel. He would have done well to keep his *Great Expectations* in check, however, when she invited him to have drinks with her and her friends.

Follow the same path you were on as it completes a semi-circle out of the park. You should emerge on Avenue A and St. Mark's Place. Turn left and head south on Avenue A one block, and make a right on 7th Street. Head west on 7th Street until you reach McSorley's Old Ale House, one of the oldest pubs in New York, between Second and Third Avenues, on your right.

9. McSorley's Old Ale House. 7 East 15th Street. He went on a date with Susan (Annabella Sciorra) and her daughter Bonnie (Christina Ricci) and afterwards, Lieutenant John Moss (James Woods) did what any self-respecting male would do: He went to a bar to drink away his sorrows and lick his wounds. And in his downtrodden state, the last person he wanted to see was actor Nick Lang (Michael J. Fox), who had been tagging along to learn about police work for an upcoming movie role, in *The Hard Way*. But Nick

showed that, although he was all thumbs when it came to police work, he did know a little bit about women.

Tour 11

Continue west on 7th and turn left on Bowery. Head south on Bowery, make a right on 4th Street and head west the short distance until you are in front of 23 East 4th Street.

10. 23 East 4th Street (between Bowery and Lafayette). Jane (Ashley Judd) and Ray (Greg Kinnear) both worked for the Diane Roberts Show, which starred Diane Roberts (Ellen Barkin) and taped in the studio located here, in *Someone Like You*. Against her better judgment and despite all her studying of the male animal, Jane found herself in an amorous relationship with Ray. And when it soured, she still had to see him every day at work.

Head back the other way on East 4th Street to the far side of Bowery. Turn right on Bowery and head south until you are in front of CBGB (OMFUG), the venerable punk rock hangout, between 2nd Street and Bleecker Street.

11. CBGB (OMFUG). 315 Bowery. It was the summer of 1977, and a madman was on the loose, killing people as they sat in parked cars. But during the *Summer of Sam*, people could feel the beat and they had to keep dancing, so they went out and tried to maintain as normal a life as possible. On a typically hot night, a nervous Vinnie (John Leguziamo) and his wife Dionna (Mira Sorvino) came here to see their friend Richie (Adrien Brody), who was one of the musical acts on the bill. But they lived in the world of disco, and as this, the heart of the punk scene, was just a little too weird for them, they got in their car and headed for greener pastures (see **Walking Tour 8**, Location 19).

Continue south on Bowery and turn left on the near side of East Houston Street. Walk east until you reach the near side of First Avenue. Cross East Houston and when you get to the south side of the street, turn left and continue east the short distance to Orchard Street. There should be a small restaurant on the southeast corner of Houston and Orchard.

12. Bereket Turkish Kebab House. 187 East Houston Street. She had doused the Fire Marshal with water, which put her in hot water with her boss, the owner of the Coyote Ugly bar. To make amends, she had to raise $250 in two hours to cover the fine. Although Kevin (Adam Garcia) liked her, Violet Sanford (Piper

Perabo) had no choice but to auction him off to the highest female bidder, which she did, with stunning results, in *Coyote Ugly*. The next day she had to make amends to Kevin, which she did by agreeing to have breakfast with him. They bought food here, then sat on the roof of his car and ushered in a new day and their new beginning.

Turn right on Orchard Street and walk south three blocks. Turn left on Delancey and walk east three blocks, until you reach Ratner's Deli, at 138 Delancey.

13. Ratner's Deli. 138 Delancey Street (at Norfolk Street). In one of his many efforts to make peace with his father, a stern and respected judge (Ron Rifkin), rogue stockbroker Seth (Giovanni Ribisi) joined his family here for dinner. But the evening quickly turned confrontational when their differences became apparent: The judge had his own ideas of what was best for his son, while Seth insisted he was better off working in the *Boiler Room*.

Look to the Williamsburg Bridge, just to the east at the end of Delancey Street, and imagine the neighborhood to the north, back in times when New York was younger and wilder.

14. Neighborhood in the Shadow of the Williamsburg Bridge. Most gangs have a "turf" they consider their own, and the young friends who grew up in the shadow of the Williamsburg Bridge considered this neighborhood theirs. And when they grew into the likes of Robert De Niro and James Woods, they ran things as if it was their office, from which they ruled with fists of steel. It was the turn of the 20th century in New York and it was *Once Upon a Time in America.*

Retrace your steps on Delancey Street. When you reach Chrystie Street (7 short blocks away), slow down and walk a bit further until you reach The Bowery Ballroom, on the north side of the street just east of Bowery.

Tour 11

15. The Bowery Ballroom. 6 Delancey Street, just east of Bowery. The owners of this club loved her tape and decided to give her a chance to sing here. En route, she had second thoughts but showed up anyway, with all her friends in the crowd. It was a far cry from *Coyote Ugly*, but here, Violet (Piper Perabo) made her musical debut.

Turn back the other way on Delancey and make a left on Chrystie Street. Head north on Chrystie the short distance until you reach Sammy's Roumanian Restaurant, on your left, at 157 Chrystie Street.

16. Sammy's Roumanian Restaurant. 157 Chrystie Street. He owned a greasy spoon in an outer borough, but Alby (Elliott Gould) wanted to make his future on the other side of the Brooklyn Bridge. After getting his Uncle Benjamin (Sid Caesar) to agree to front him the money to buy a restaurant in Manhattan, Alby and his entire family came here to celebrate the new venture. But, for Alby, crossing *Over the Brooklyn Bridge* came with a heavy price: his uncle wanted him to dump his non-Jewish girlfriend, Elizabeth (Margaux Hemingway). The dinner started amicably, but Alby finally decided to stand up for what he believed in, and what was in his heart, and he set the family straight about a whole host of issues. After the dirty laundry was exposed, much to the chagrin of the restaurant's other patrons, it seemed like the family was finally heading in the right direction, and Alby would get to keep his restaurant, and his girlfriend.

You have now reached the end of **Walking Tour 11: The Lower East Side**.

SAVOY
SAVOY

Walking Tour 12

CULTURE CLASH CORRIDOR

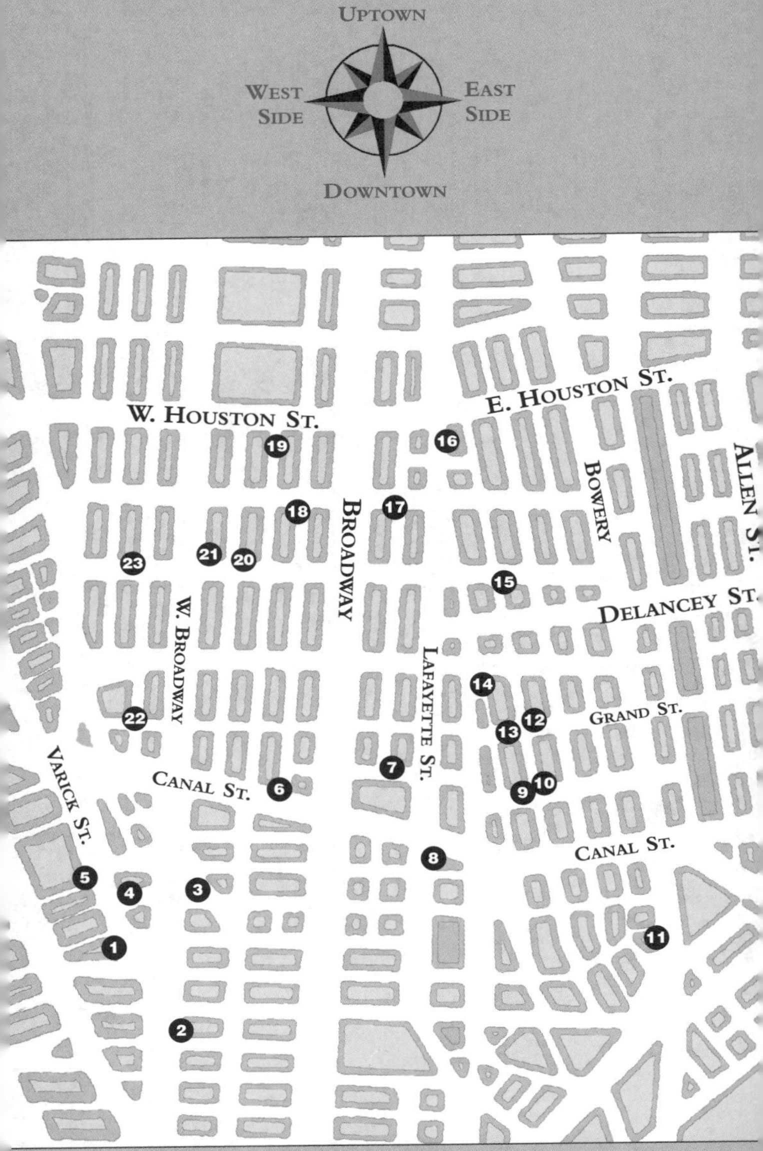

W. HOUSTON ST.
E. HOUSTON ST.
BOWERY
ALLEN ST.
BROADWAY
DELANCEY ST.
W. BROADWAY
LAFAYETTE ST.
GRAND ST.
VARICK ST.
CANAL ST.
CANAL ST.

16 19 17 18 21 20 23 15 14 12 13 22 7 6 10 9 8 5 4 3 11 1 2

Walking Tour 12

Culture Clash Corridor

As the name signifies, **Walking Tour 12: Culture Clash Corridor** covers the greatest diversity of cultures, ethnicities, lifestyles and tastes, all within a relatively small geographical area. One neighborhood literally begins where another leaves off, giving this part of Manhattan the feel of a real-life Disneyland, where you turn the corner from Little Italy and find yourself in Chinatown. Unlike Disneyland, however, the people and the attractions here are real.

Walking Tour 12: Culture Clash Corridor begins at the intersection of Franklin Street and Varick Street. If you choose to get to the starting point by public transportation, you may use any of the following subway or bus lines (although the following list is by no means exhaustive):

FROM THE NORTH

Subways

- **1** or **2** southbound to Franklin Street.
- **3** southbound to 14th Street. Switch to **1** or **2** southbound to Franklin Street.
- **A**, **C** or **E** southbound to Canal Street. Walk south on West Broadway, to Franklin Street.

Buses

- **M20** southbound on Seventh Avenue, then Seventh Avenue South, then Varick Street to Franklin Street.

FROM THE SOUTH

SUBWAYS

- **1** or **2** northbound to Franklin Street.

FROM THE EAST

SUBWAYS

- **A**, **C** or **E** westbound to Canal Street. Walk south on West Broadway, to Franklin Street.

BUSES

- **M21** southbound on Avenue C, then westbound on Houston Street, to Avenue of the Americas. Transfer to **M20** southbound on Varick Street, to Franklin Street.

If you took the subway to Franklin Street, you walked up this beautiful and ornate stairway that would probably be more fitting on the streets of Paris than those of New York. However you got here, stand near the entrance without getting in the way of rushing commuters.

1. Franklin Street Subway Entrance (at Varick). They were both involved with others, but nothing was going to get in the way of true love. Or at least, true passion. Or maybe it was

simply lust. They were used to traveling in a world peopled by celebrities, so they decided to do as those around them did. In *Celebrity*, Lee

Simon (Kenneth Branagh) and Nola (Winona Ryder) threw caution to the wind and had a rendezvous late one night in front of these stairs.

Head east on Franklin (away from Varick) and make a right on West Broadway. Go south on West Broadway three blocks until you reach Thomas Street. The restaurant Odeon will be on the southeast corner of Thomas and West Broadway.

2. Odeon. 145 West Broadway (at Thomas Street). A fixture of nightlife in the 1980's, Odeon is the place that Seth (Giovanni Ribisi) and the other brokers from the shadowy firm of J.T. Marlin came to celebrate their good fortunes, and got into an argument during dinner, with other brokers who didn't think all that much of them, in *Boiler Room*.

Turn back north on West Broadway until you reach White Street. A coffee shop should be on the northeast corner of West Broadway and White.

3. 235 West Broadway (at White Street). Although my friend Alejandro insists that the coffee shop in *It Could Happen to You* was actually constructed on a vacant lot at West Broadway and North Moore (and then dismantled soon after), and he goes so far as to claim he watched this construction take place during his lunch breaks, the one you see in the movie looks an awful lot like the one right here. So, for our purposes, this is the one we will talk about. In the movie, Yvonne (Bridget Fonda) was a waitress in the coffee shop and Charlie (Nicolas Cage) a police officer who walked a nearby beat. And when Charlie didn't have enough money to leave a nice tip, he told Yvonne he would share his lottery winnings with her, if he actually won. And wouldn't you know it, he did. True to his word, he split the winnings, and that was the beginning of the end for Charlie and his less altruistic wife, Muriel (Rosie Perez).

Continue the short distance north to North Moore Street and make a left. Walk west on North Moore until you reach the firehouse on the left, just before the corner of Varick Street.

4. Hook & Ladder 8. Varick and North Moore Streets. True, this location appeared in *Manhattan on Film* (**Walking Tour 12,** Location 16), but that's because it was the home of the ghostbusting trio of Peter (Bill Murray), Ray (Dan Aykroyd) and Egon (Harold Ramis), in *Ghostbusters*. It appears in this volume, because they resurrected their ghostbusting activities and continued to operate out of this location, in *Ghostbusters II*. Pretty lame reasoning, I admit, but it's such a great location, I couldn't resist including it again. More important, it is an appropriate place to offer a prayer for the firemen who perished in the World Trade Center attacks on September 11, 2001.

Now turn right on Varick and walk north one block, to Ericsson Place. You will find the venerated 1st Precinct located on the southwest corner of Varick and Ericsson Place.

5. 1st Precinct. Varick Street and Ericsson Place. Madmen were on the loose, terrorizing the city, capturing it all on video and hoping to get their *15 Minutes* of fame. But the authorities were hot on their trail. Arson investigator Jordy Warsaw (Ed Burns) brought Daphne (Vera Farmiga), the only witness to a double homicide, here and traded ideas with Detective Eddie Flemming (Robert De Niro). Afterwards, to avoid the frenzy-feeding media outside the front door, they left through a side door, further away from Varick Street.

After pausing yet again, this time to remember the police who were among the true American heroes in the aftermath of the World Trade Center attacks, find Walker Street, which is behind you to your left. Head east on Walker (away from the 1st Precinct) and then turn left on Church Street. Head north on Church and turn right on Canal Street. Head east and stop across from Pearl Paint, at the corner of Canal and Mercer Streets.

6. Across from Pearl Paint. 308 Canal Street (at Mercer Street). Each day can be a struggle for an aspiring actor and playwright, what with trips to the copy store, the stationery store and the post office. But on one particular day for Wallace Shawn (portraying himself), his typical activities seemed like a welcome breeze compared to what his evening held: dinner with an old friend and mentor, Andre Gregory. Worrying about whether it would be among the most boring evenings he had ever spent, Shawn crossed Canal Street near Pearl Paint and headed for the subway, and his dinner date in *My Dinner With Andre*.

Continue east on Canal, turn left on Broadway and head north one block. Make a right on Howard Street and stop at the building on the northeast corner of Howard and Crosby Streets.

7. 28 Howard Street (northeast corner at Crosby). Mild-mannered word processor Paul Hackett (Griffin Dunne) led a pretty boring existence, so when he met the beautiful and alluring Marcy (Rosanna Arquette) at a coffee shop, he decided a change in routine might do him some good. How wrong he turned out to be. Later in the evening he called Marcy and arranged to meet her downtown, *After Hours*, for what can only be described as a wild and bizarre evening of paranoia, mayhem and death. The nightmare began innocently enough, in Marcy's loft, which was inside this building, where she lived with Kiki Bridges (Linda Fiorentino). By morning, Paul was happy to return to his boring job in his boring world, far uptown.

While facing Marcy and Kiki's building, turn right and continue east on Howard Street. Turn right on Lafayette Street and walk south to the south side of Canal Street. Stand near the entrance to the subway station on the southeast corner of Canal and Lafayette Streets.

8. Canal Street Subway Entrance. Southeast corner of Canal and Lafayette Streets. It was not the Thanksgiving Day Dr. Nathan Conrad (Michael Douglas) had been hoping for, having begun with the kidnapping of his daughter. A few hours later, Dr. Conrad had whisked his greatly troubled *pro bono* patient, 18-year-old Elisabeth Burrows (Brittany Murphy) out of the Bridgeview Psychiatric Hospital and the two of them paused at the top of these stairs, anticipating with dread what lay below. For Elisabeth, it was the prospect of reliving the horror she had witnessed ten years before and for Dr. Conrad, in *Don't Say a Word*, it was a necessary step toward getting his daughter back unharmed. Knowing the enormity of the stakes for both of them, they worked their way down the steps and onto the platform of the subway station below.

Head east on Canal Street (away from Lafayette) and turn left on Centre Street. Head north on Centre and turn right on Hester Street. Walk east a bit on Hester until you can soak up the old world flavor. If you reach Mulberry Street, stop there.

9. Hester Street. America said to "Give me your tired, your poor" and they came. From all over the world, but, initially, mainly from places in Europe to a land where they hoped to make lives for themselves that were better than those they had left behind. If they were lucky, they might even realize the American dream, which differed for every person who landed on our shores. From Eastern Europe, a huge number of Jewish people fled tyranny, poverty and pogroms and settled here, in the New York brought to life in *Hester Street*. That is exactly what Gitl (Carol Kane), whose husband had come here first, did. But while the neighborhood tried its best to replicate the culture of their homeland, it didn't succeed on all fronts, and the immigrants on and around Hester Street were introduced to something much less common back home: divorce.

If you have not yet reached Mulberry Street, continue east until you get there.

10. Hester and Mulberry Streets. Because it's a private social club, I can't really tell you where it was, but it was somewhere in the vicinity of this intersection and Rossi (Tom Berenger) came here to try and make the City a better place, in *Fear City*.

Continue east on Hester and make a right on Mott Street. After you pass Bayard Street, make the next left onto Pell Street. Halfway down Pell, turn right onto Doyers Street, one of the most striking streets in Manhattan. Stop in front of 15-17 Doyers, which will be on your right.

11. 15-17 Doyers Street. Proving that a small time crook will always be a small time crook, Ray (Woody Allen) wasn't satisfied making money the old fashioned way. Never really happy, even after his wife's cookie business made them millionaires, Ray hatched a scheme to steal a priceless piece of jewelry from one of his high society acquaintances. In *Small Time Crooks*, Ray came here to pick up the replica of the expensive jewelry that was made for him, in hopes of swapping the fake for the original. Being small-time, Ray did very little right.

Continue to the end of Doyers and make a left on Bowery. Walk north on Bowery and turn left on Grand Street. Walk west on Grand and stop when you reach Mulberry Street.

12. Mulberry and Grand Streets. Northeast corner. They were late for their dinner reservation but Gina (Jeanne Tripplehorn) had to stop, because Michael (Hugh Grant) was running in such a silly way that he was making her laugh too hard. She begged him to run normally, but when the man who would become known as *Mickey Blue Eyes* told her with his patented puppy dog look of despair that he had been running normally, and that he was hurt by her comment, it pretty much set the tone for the evening.

If you haven't figured it out yet, you are in the part of New York known as Little Italy.

13. Little Italy. Although no doubt recreated on a set to look like the Little Italy of New York at the beginning of the 20th century, the flavor of this neighborhood was brilliantly captured in *Godfather Part II*, as the young Vito Corleone (Robert De Niro), Clemenza (Bruno Kirby, Jr.) and others learned the craft of making a living on the streets, using their guile and wits.

Continue west on Grand Street and make a right on Centre Street. Head north on Centre until you reach 240 Centre Street.

14. 240 Centre Street. This building is now the address of some pretty ritzy condominiums, but in earlier days in New York, as well as in *Madigan*, it was the central police headquarters,

and where the offices of Police Commissioner Anthony Russell (Henry Fonda) were located.

Continue north on Centre Street, then make a right on Broome Street and a quick left on Mulberry Street. Walk north on Mulberry until you reach Spring Street. There should be a small playground on the southeast corner of Mulberry and Spring.

Tour 12

15. Playground at Mulberry and Spring. Charlie (Mickey Rourke) was *The Pope of Greenwich Village*, but he spent a good amount of time down here, on the northern fringes of Little Italy. During one of many conversations held in this playground, Diane (Daryl Hannah) begged Charlie not to go, even though she had no idea where he was going.

Keep going north on Mulberry and make a left on Prince Street. Head west on Prince, turn right on Lafayette Street and go north until you reach the Puck Building, south of Houston.
You are now in the neighborhood known as SoHo.

16. The Puck Building. 295 Lafayette Street. This beautiful building is home to the office of Grace Adler (Debra Messing) in the Emmy-winning television show "Will and Grace."

Head back south on Lafayette and make a right on the south side of Prince Street. Walk west on Prince. At the corner of Crosby Street, you will see the restaurant Savoy on your left. Walk to the corner and look south (to your left) on Crosby Street.

17. Crosby Street, just south of Savoy (at 70 Prince Street). Gwen (Sandra Bullock) had made it through the *28 Days* of rehab and was hoping to get her life back on track. But to keep her alcoholism in check, Gwen knew she would have to put behind her not only her drinking days but certain friends and lovers as well. As she turned the corner in front of the Savoy, right where you are now standing, Gwen saw her boyfriend Jasper (Dominic West) sitting on the stoop of her building, which was a short distance down Crosby Street. Jasper was hoping that they could go back to the way things had been, but Gwen knew that she had to make a clean break.

Continue west on Prince. One block past Broadway, you will come to Mercer Street. Note Fanelli's, the longstanding eatery on the southwest corner of Prince and Mercer.

18. Fanelli's. 94 Prince Street (at Mercer). While his gang watched from a nearby vantage point, Frankie (Ed Harris) had a sit-down here with Borelli (Joe Viterelli). The meeting put Frankie in a state of panic because the topic of discussion was how best to deal with Frankie's brother Jackie (a typically out-of-control Gary Oldman). In *State of Grace*, Borelli told Frankie to "solve" the problem, or else it would be solved for him.

Continue west on Prince and turn right on Greene Street. Walk north on Greene until you reach Kelley & Ping, at 127 Greene, on the west side of the street.

19. Kelley & Ping. 127 Greene Street (between Prince and Houston). He left a formal cocktail party that was largely in his honor, and raced through the streets of Manhattan in the pouring rain. When he got to this restaurant, he stormed inside and interrupted Estella (Gwyneth Paltrow), who was having dinner with her fiancé, Walter (Hank Azaria) and some others, and asked her to dance. Forsaking the others, Estella danced with Finn (Ethan Hawke) and then left the restaurant with him. They barely made it to his loft, in *Great Expectations*, before they finally consummated the passion that had been simmering between them, unspoken, for years.

Head back south on Greene and turn right on Spring Street. Walk west one block to Wooster Street. Our next location is on the northeast corner of Spring and Wooster.

20. 139 Spring Street (at Wooster). Several years after figuring out how to deal with his brother Jackie in *State of Grace*, Ed Harris was figuring out how best to deal with another Jackie, in this case, his ex-wife. In *Stepmom*, Luke (Ed Harris) had divorced Jackie (Susan Sarandon), the mother of his children, and was planning to marry a much younger woman, Isabel (Julia Roberts), which made his ex feel anything but warm and fuzzy. Having left his house in the suburbs, Luke was ready for a change and lived in a loft in this building with his young fiancée.

Continue west on Spring Street and turn right on West Broadway. Look for OTP (Otto Tootsi Plohound) at 413 West Broadway, on the east side of the street.

21. OTP. 413 West Broadway (between Spring and Prince Streets). With time running out on his mission, Nicky (Adam Sandler) began approaching people in the street, trying to lure them into the special flask he had been given. In *Little Nicky*, he even pulled a man off a passing bicycle in front of this store. The man beat him mercilessly before continuing on his way.

Turn south on West Broadway (OTP will be on your left) and walk south past Spring and Broome Streets. Turn right on Grand Street and walk west. Stop at Thompson Street. Note the restaurant across Thompson, on the northwest corner of the intersection of Thompson and Grand.

22. Café Noir. 32 Grand Street (at Thompson). People write letters to erotic magazines about such encounters, but Constance Sumner (Diane Lane) was going to keep this one to herself. After unexpectedly running into some friends while on the way to one of her passion sessions with rare book dealer Paul Martel (Olivier Martinez) and finding herself stuck with "the girls" at a table just inside this popular SoHo gathering place, she was thrilled to see her illicit paramour show up and head for the bathrooms in the back of the restaurant. Excusing herself, Constance followed him and, moments later, she and Paul had a wild sexual encounter while her friends waited for her. Afterwards, slightly disheveled from her tryst but happy nonetheless, Constance sat with her friends and they engaged in a discussion of the pitfalls of being *Unfaithful*. Her friends didn't realize how close to Constance's home the discussion was actually hitting.

Turn to the right and walk north on Thompson Street, a few blocks until you are in front of SoHo Laundry, at 101 Thompson Street.

23. 101 Thompson Street, near Spring. He was about to be married and for a professional football player with a pretty large following, that was a pretty big deal. While his friends looked on, ready to rib him mercilessly, Lance (Morris Chestnut) signed autographs, flirted with and charmed the daylights out of a small group of female admirers. After he shared a few moments with his fans in front of this store, Lance and his friends, in *The Best Man*, walked north.

You have now reached the end of **Walking Tour 12: Culture Clash Corridor.**

Walking Tour 13

America's Heart

UPTOWN
WEST SIDE
EAST SIDE
DOWNTOWN
CANAL ST. 
LAFAYETTE ST.
CENTRE ST.
CANAL ST.
HUDSON ST.
GREENWICH ST.
WEST BROADWAY
BROADWAY
PARK ROW
CHAMBERS ST.
CITY HALL
FULTON ST.
FULTON ST.
CHURCH ST.
WALL ST.
EXCHANGE PL.
WATER ST.
BROAD ST.
BATTERY PL.
STATE ST.
WHITEHALL ST.
1
2
3
4
5
6
7
8
9
10
11
12
13
14
15
16
17
18
19
20
21
22
23
24
25
26
27
28
29
30
31
32

Walking Tour 13

America's Heart

Geographically, the actual heart of America might be somewhere closer to Indianapolis, Indiana, but for reasons that will soon become clear, that phrase is an apt description of downtown Manhattan.

When I began work on *Manhattan on Film 2*, it had been my intention to describe **Walking Tour 13** in a manner similar to the way I described the corresponding tour in *Manhattan on Film*—Downtown and Financial District—for that is what this southern tip of Manhattan has been for most of the 20th century. But that was before the morning of September 11, 2001, when we learned, once and for all, how life can change in the blink of an eye.

The terrorist attacks on the World Trade Center in lower Manhattan—which culminated in death and destruction to a degree never before seen in this country and for which the proper word to describe the horror has not yet been found—have forever changed the landscape of a nation. Beyond the physical structures that stand no more and the thousands of lives that were brutally brought to a catastrophic end, the fallout will affect us all for the rest of our lives, because on that day, America, if not the world, lost whatever remained of its innocence.

Witnesses to the unforgettable events of September 11, 2001, compared the unfolding scene to one that seemed more appropriate in a movie, and those of us who were lucky enough to be nowhere near the World Trade Center that day but still unlucky enough to witness everything through the ubiquitous live TV coverage, could only marvel how apt that description seemed to be. Of course, the fact that it wasn't a movie made the horror that much greater.

I had originally intended to scout downtown locations for this book on the morning of September 11th, and I probably would have been pretty close to the World Trade Center when the planes hit. As luck would have it, Jaden, my then six-day-old son, kept Ashley and me up most of the night, which caused me to delay my original early morning departure. As parents, it is our job to protect our kids. In a wonderful twist, at such a tender age, Jaden protected me. And for that, I will always be grateful.

September 11, 2001, and in the period that has followed, all of America, as well as most of the rest of the world, has rallied to support us. If, as the old saying goes, "all roads lead to Rome," in this case, "all eyes look to downtown Manhattan." And while it has become known as "Ground Zero" in the aftermath of the attacks, it is also the focal point, the reminder, the rallying cry, from which America will draw its strength to carry on and somehow, emerge wiser, stronger and greater. And it is for that reason that I consider downtown Manhattan to be America's Heart.

Needless to say, the terrorists destroyed some past and future movie locations on September 11, and filmmakers in the days and years to come will feel the loss of the full richness that America's Heart once offered. But the films that used the World Trade Center and its environs in the past will help to etch those buildings, and what they stood for, in our memories, minds and hearts.

In light of the terrorist attacks, **Walking Tour 13: America's Heart** begins fittingly enough, at the Criminal Court House in lower Manhattan. If you choose to get to the starting point by public transportation, you may use any of the following subway or bus lines (although the following list is by no means exhaustive):

FROM THE NORTH

SUBWAYS

- **6** southbound to Canal Street. Walk south on Centre Street to 100 Centre.
- **4** or **5** southbound to 14th Street. Transfer to **6** southbound to Canal Street. Walk south on Centre Street to 100 Centre.

BUSES

- **M6** southbound on Seventh Avenue, then Broadway, to Leonard Street. Walk east on Leonard to Centre Street.

FROM THE SOUTH

SUBWAYS

- **6** northbound to Canal Street. Walk south on Centre Street to 100 Centre.

FROM THE EAST

BUSES

- **M9** westbound on East Broadway, then Park Row, to Centre Street. Walk north on Centre Street to 100 Centre.
- **M22** westbound on Madison Street [not Madison Avenue], then Park Row, to Centre Street. Walk north on Centre Street to 100 Centre.

The Criminal Courthouse is located at 100 Centre Street, just north of Hogan Place.

1. Criminal Courthouse. 100 Centre Street. This building was the focus of the A & E television series and its address gave the series its name. It is the actual criminal courthouse for the entire borough of Manhattan, and it is where the trial of Mr. Hoover (Anthony Hopkins) took place. Mr. Hoover believed that his daughter, *Audrey Rose*, killed in a car crash, had been reincarnated into the body of a 12-year-old girl named Ivy Templeton (Susan Swift), and when Ivy's parents didn't go along with him, he took custody of the girl and was subsequently charged with kidnapping.

And prior to that, 100 Centre Street is where assistant district attorney Adam Bonner (Spencer Tracy) prosecuted Doris Attinger (Judy Holliday), who was accused of the attempted murder of her husband. What made this case such a thorn in Bonner's side was that the defendant's counsel was Amanda Bonner (Katherine Hepburn), who was also Bonner's wife, in *Adam's Rib*.

Head south on Centre Street, past Worth Street, until you are in front of the New York County Supreme Court, at 60 Centre Street.

2. Supreme Court. 60 Centre Street. Although more often the venue of civil cases rather than criminal, 60 Centre Street is where the dedicated jurors, among them Henry Fonda, Ed Begley, E.G. Marshall, Jack Klugman and Martin Balsam, spent some agonizing hours trying to decide the fate of a young man accused of murder, in *12 Angry Men*.

After being cleared of all charges against him, former fugitive Mark Sheridan (Wesley Snipes) left a press conference held on the steps of this courthouse, bid farewell to Deputy Marshal Sam Gerard (Tommy Lee Jones) who had led his team of *U.S. Marshals* in Mark's pursuit, and descended these steps to freedom.

Turn from the courthouse and look west across Centre Street. There is a small park called Thomas Paine Park and there are numerous benches in the park.

3. Bench just west of 60 Centre Street. He wasn't sure that marriage was for him, but Norma

(Pier Angeli) loved him and that was a wonderful thing. While trying to decide whether to go across the street and get a marriage license, Rocky Graziano (Paul Newman) and Norma sat on a bench here and wrestled with the problem. In *Somebody Up There Likes Me*, Rocky realized that somebody down here liked him, too. And he decided to do something about it.

Continue south on Centre Street. You will pass Pearl Street and should continue until you are in front of the magnificent structure on your left, the Municipal Building.

4. The Municipal Building. 1 Centre Street. They had only known each other a day, but they knew it was right. Also, the clock was ticking and Joe (Robert Walker) didn't have much time left on his leave in New York City. So, in *The Clock*, Joe and Alice (Judy Garland) came here to get married.

Police officer Mike Brennan (Nick Nolte) had shot a man and assistant district attorney Al Reilly (Timothy Hutton) was assigned to the case. Reilly had lots of questions but very few answers, and he did not yet know that he might be in over his head. In *Q & A*, a number of conversations took place in front of this building.

Cross Centre Street, heading away from the Municipal Building. Walk west on the north side of Chambers Street and stop in front of the Surrogate Court House, at 31 Chambers Street.

5. Surrogates Court. 31 Chambers Street. Dora (Mena Suvari) was no loser, but she was in a tough spot. Because her parents' income was too high, she did not qualify for financial aid to attend college, which she did here in New York. But she wasn't making enough money at her job to cover tuition. So Dora came here to see about getting a second job. In *Loser*, this building housed the school's financial aid office, although in actuality it is the Surrogates Court. If the building is open and you have time, go in and look around. You will see why they do so much filming in the first-floor lobby and on the staircase leading to the second floor.

In *Great Expectations*, there was a fancy party and Finn (Ethan Hawke) showed up fashionably late. The party was held here and Finn was the guest of honor, but he had more on his mind than art, even if the art was his, and idle cocktail party chatter. With thoughts only of Estella (Gwyneth Paltrow), Finn quickly left the party and ran through the rain-soaked Manhattan streets, hoping to find her. He did (see **Walking Tour 12**, Location 19).

Return to Centre Street and make a right. When you get to the south side of Chambers, continue south, but keep glancing to your left until you get a good view of the Brooklyn Bridge, standing proudly behind the Municipal Building.

6. Brooklyn Bridge. Built more than a hundred years ago and still going strong, the Brooklyn Bridge is one of the most recognizable structures in all of Manhattan (a picture of it adorns the back cover of *Manhattan on Film*). Because of its beauty and longevity, it is not surprising that the bridge has served as a backdrop in so many films over the years. Even Tarzan has scaled its cables and beams. In *Tarzan's New York Adventure*, Tarzan (Johnny Weissmuller) was a long way from home and forced to fit his muscular physique uncomfortably into a suit. But that didn't stop him from climbing the cables of this bridge right to the top, while the police gave chase. But Tarzan was a breed apart and as the cops inched closer and capture seemed imminent, he dove into the waters of the East River below.

Nebraska attorney Jerry Ryan (Robert Mitchum) chose a much more civilized method of crossing the bridge. Moving to New York after his divorce, he bypassed the cables and beams and strolled along the center of the bridge as he crossed into Manhattan at the start of his new life and the beginning of *Two For the Seesaw*.

Tour 13

Sophie (Meryl Streep) also walked along the bridge, but her past was a lot more terrifying than Jerry Ryan's. She had been in the Holocaust, and New York represented not only freedom but an opportunity to try and forget the horrors she had endured. One night, she, Nathan (Kevin Kline) and their friend Stingo (Peter MacNicol) walked across the bridge, opening a bottle of champagne to celebrate along the way. They toasted Stingo as the next great American writer, but at the end of *Sophie's Choice*, Stingo crossed the legendary span alone, as a new day beckoned.

Literary success may have eluded Stingo, but not Ivan Travalian (Al Pacino). His play was being mounted on Broadway; it was his love life that wasn't in the greatest shape. After his wife left him, Ivan figured he'd be going it alone, but then Alice Detroit (Dyan Cannon) came into his life like a hurricane and in *Author! Author!* the two of them strolled along the bridge.

As Ivan and Alice walked, they no doubt had to step aside to allow John/Judas (David Haskell) to pass, as he headed across the bridge, wheeling his multi-colored cart into Manhattan to gather the other free-spirits, at the start of the rock opera *Godspell*.

And back in the days when the Brooklyn Bridge was under construction, 1876 to be exact, Leopold Alexis, Duke of Albany (Hugh Jackman), followed Stuart (Liev Schreiber) onto the bridge and through a time machine of sorts, into modern-day New York. There a creature like none he had ever before encountered awaited him: the modern, New York woman, packaged nicely in the form of Kate McKay (Meg Ryan), in *Kate and Leopold*.

You can't see it from here, and it's probably no longer there, but many years ago, there was a shack under the Brooklyn Bridge on the Manhattan side, which offered live bait and shelter from the rain.

7. Shack Under the Brooklyn Bridge. Skip McCoy (Richard Widmark) lived in just such a shack in *Pickup on South Street*. The shack advertised "Live Bait" and "Fishing Tackle for Rent," and Skip received more than his fair share of visitors. But the traffic increased dramatically after Skip lifted a wallet from the purse of a stranger on the subway. But when that stranger, Candy (Jean Peters), and others started coming by looking for microfilm that had been in the wallet, Skip realized that he may have chosen the wrong wallet to steal.

From his shack, Skip may have gotten a great view of a boat passing under the bridge.

8. Boat on East River, under Brooklyn Bridge. In the boat, Skip might have seen Hazel Flagg (Carole Lombard), who, supposedly dying of some mysterious ailment and in New York for a whirlwind "last gasp" around the city, was being shown the sights by crack reporter, Wallace Cook (Fredric March). Of course, in *Nothing Sacred*, if Cook had been such an ace, he should have gotten to the truth about Hazel sooner, but, as the old saying goes, love is blind.

Also on the water, but moving somewhat more slowly on a tugboat, were Aaron (William Fichtner) and Martha (Demi Moore). While they cruised the East River and passed under the Brooklyn Bridge, Aaron declared the bridge to be his favorite, in *Passion of Mind*.

It is now time to turn away from the Brooklyn Bridge and leave it to be admired by others. Continue south on Centre Street and stop at the top of the subway stairs that are just up ahead.

9. Centre Street Subway Stairs, across from Brooklyn Bridge. Actor Nick Lang (Michael J. Fox) came to New York to find out what the life of an authentic New York City cop was like. And authentic New York City cop John Moss (James Woods) drew the short straw and had to let Nick tag along as he went about his day. But Nick soon learned *The Hard Way* that portraying a cop in the movies was much safer than being a cop in real life. He was pinned down by gunfire on the subway platform and John Moss had to come to the rescue, which he did by racing down this staircase.

Continue your southward journey as Centre Street becomes Park Row. Keep walking until City Hall comes into clear view on your right. Get a good look at its front steps.

10. City Hall. Park Row. He won the lottery, and that can happen to anyone. But when he put his life on the line to thwart a robbery attempt in a grocery store, the entire city shared in his success. For his efforts, police officer Charlie (Nicolas Cage) received a citation for bravery on the steps of City Hall, in *It Could Happen to You*.

Cross Park Row (away from City Hall) at your earliest, and safest, opportunity, and continue heading south. When you reach Beekman Street, turn left and walk east. At Nassau Street, turn and look in the direction from which you just came. The shining elegance of the Woolworth Building should loom overhead, on the west side of City Hall Park.

11. Woolworth Building (viewed from intersection of Nassau and Beekman Streets). When Billy Bathgate (Loren Dean) stood at this intersection, in *Billy Bathgate*, he gazed in awe at the splendor of the Woolworth Building. His awe would soon find another recipient in the person of Dutch Schultz, but unlike the mobster, the magnificence of this building remains to this day.

Turn left and head south on Nassau Street. Continue to the south side of Liberty Street and turn left. The Federal Reserve Building should be just in front of you and slightly to your left.

12. Federal Reserve Building. William and

Liberty Streets. Although stuck in bed with a nasty cold (see **Walking Tour 7,** Location 21), the Mayor (Lee Wallace) was still in charge. Willing to meet the demands of the hijackers who had taken over a subway train, the Mayor, in order to save the lives of the hostages on board, authorized the payment of $1,000,000 to be made to the perpetrators, in *The Taking of Pelham One, Two, Three*. With only minutes to go before the deadline, the police gathered the money in this building, placed it into a police car and sped off to get to the subway car in time (see **Walking Tour 9**, Location 7).

Continue south on Nassau Street. When you reach Wall Street, take a good look at the pillars of the New York Stock Exchange across Wall and slightly to the right.

13. New York Stock Exchange. 20 Broad Street. Although Eugene (Ron Silver) seemed like a normal guy by day, working on "the Exchange" as a trader, he was leading a double life that was becoming more of a headache for New York. As his nighttime activities increasingly turned to murder, the police stepped up their efforts to nab him, and police officer Megan Turner (Jamie Lee Curtis) made his capture her number one priority, in *Blue Steel*. Megan had a special interest in finding the killer since Eugene had obtained his gun during a supermarket robbery attempt in which Megan had interceded.

Cross to the south side of Wall Street and turn around. 14 Wall should be on the corner diagonally across Wall Street from where you are standing.

14. 14 Wall Street. On an otherwise deserted Wall Street in the early hours of a new day, Murray Burns (Jason Robards) and Sandra (Barbara

Harris) walked along and stopped in front of 14 Wall, realizing that the two of them were all alone, surrounded by all the money that these buildings represented, in *A Thousand Clowns*.

From where you stand, you can see the Federal Building (with the statue of George Washington in front) directly across Wall Street. Look for a sewer plate in the street, between you and the Federal Building.

15. Sewer Plate on Wall Street, in Front of Federal Building. Another serial killer was at large, and this one was even more devious than Eugene from *Blue Steel*. The city's best hope in tracking him down was a quadriplegic, Link (Denzel Washington), confined to bed and unable to do anything for himself. But Link was intent on catching this madman, *The Bone Collector*, and he enlisted the help of an initially un-

Tour 13

cooperative young cop, Amelia (Angelina Jolie), to be his eyes and ears. With time running out, Amelia and other cops entered the sewer system through the sewer plate right in front of you, to try and find a kidnapping victim before she became a murder victim.

Turn around and head south on Broad Street. The New York Stock Exchange should be on your right. Stop when you are across from 30 Broad Street.

16. 30 Broad Street. The headquarters of Linus Larrabee (Humphrey Bogart) and his family were located in this building, in the original film version of *Sabrina*. In the remake (starring Harrison Ford), the Larrebee family's office building was located at 399 Park Avenue (see *Manhattan on Film*, **Walking Tour 7**, Location 27).

Another rich and powerful man spent some time in this building, but his fortunes quickly changed. Avery Bullard (an un-billed Raoul Freeman), the head of the Treadway Furniture Corporation, collapsed to the ground as he exited this building, and his death set off a ruthless scramble for power, high atop the company's offices, in the *Executive Suite*.

Continue south on Broad Street and turn left on Beaver Street. Head east until you reach William Street. Delmonico's should be on your right.

17. William and Beaver Streets (in front of Delmonico's). Her illness grew worse with each passing day, but her senses were more heightened than ever. As they passed this intersection in their car, Charlotte (Winona Ryder) put her hand over the heart of Will (Richard Gere) and could tell that he was lying. Realizing that he had been unfaithful and that he would never change his wild ways, Charlotte got out of the car at this spot, in *Autumn in New York*.

Turn right on William and head east until you reach Harry's of Hanover Square, which is on William, between Stone and Pearl Streets. A long-standing downtown eatery, Harry's may provide some sustenance for the rest of your journey.

18. Harry's of Hanover Square. 1 Hanover Square (between Stone and Pearl Streets). Jack Prescott (Jeff Bridges) and Dwan (Jessica Lange) sought some shelter and a drink here, in *King Kong*. With the gargantuan ape at large in New York, the town was crazed with fear and people were either fleeing from the beast's path or heading into battle with it. The place was empty, but Jack and Dwan helped themselves to drinks and enjoyed the few minutes of solitude it afforded them. Then, while sitting at a table, Jack figured out where Kong would be heading, and the two of them rushed to that destination, hoping to get there before it was too late.

Return to Beaver Street and make a right. When you reach Hanover Street, stop and you'll see Killarney Rose, a short distance down Beaver Street from Hanover, on your right.

19. Killarney Rose. 80 Beaver Street (between Hanover and Pearl Streets). This long-standing financial district watering hole has hosted many a night of drinking among the brokers, traders, bankers and lawyers who populate this part of Manhattan. In fact, some of them worked for J.T. Marlin, in *Boiler Room*.

Turn left on Hanover Street and make a quick left onto Exchange Place. Stop when you are in front of 20 Exchange Place, with the very distinct address markers astride the entrance.

20. 20 Exchange Place. This building is where the offices of the North Coast Fidelity and Casualty Company were located. It was 1940, and the insurance company, run by Mr. Magruder (Dan Aykroyd), employed such people as George Bond (Wallace Shawn), Betty Ann Fitzgerald (Helen Hunt) and C.W. Briggs (Woody Allen). And all seemed rosy, until Betty Ann and Briggsy came under *The Curse of the Jade Scorpion*.

Continue past 20 Exchange Place and turn right on William Street. Walk north on William and turn right on Wall Street. Walk east on Wall, pass Water Street and continue until you are across from 120 Wall, just west of South Street.

21. 120 Wall Street. He was a multimillionaire, but he wasn't going to tell that to Shotzy (Lauren Bacall), whose only goal was to marry for money and who had all but written the book on *How to Marry a Millionaire*. But Tom Brookman (Cameron Mitchell) was smitten nonetheless, so he was willing to chance it. And although Tom looked just like the guy next door, he was loaded and his company was located here, in the building that was named for him.

Turn right from 120 Wall Street and head south on South Street. Walk until you reach the sign that says "Exit 1, Battery Park, Staten Island" at the southern terminus of the FDR Drive. You should be in the shadows of 55 Water Street and the New York City Vietnam Veterans Memorial Plaza should be on your right.

22. South Street at Vietnam Memorial Plaza. There was something rotten among New York's Finest and Officer Frank Serpico (Al Pacino) thought he should do something about it. In *Serpico*, he decided to tell what he knew, and got into a car parked along the side of the road right around here. By talking to the higher-ups, Serpico knew he was taking his life in his hands, but he felt he was doing the right thing, and that was what mattered in the end.

Directly across the street, you will see the Downtown-Manhattan Heliport.

23. Downtown-Manhattan Heliport. At the beginning of *They All Laughed*, John (Ben Gazzara) stood near where you are standing and watched as Angela (Audrey Hepburn) emerged

from a helicopter at the Heliport. He was a private detective and he was hired to perform a service, but the lovely Angela was someone he was glad to keep an eye on.

Continue in the same direction on South Street. Keep looking to your left, out onto the water. With any luck, you might see the Staten Island Ferry making its way.

24. Staten Island Ferry. They had each other, they had their common hobby and they had their friends, but for Helen (Kitty Winn) and Bobby (Al Pacino), that wasn't enough. So they boarded the ferry and headed to Staten Island to get a puppy. But on the return trip, with their new puppy, Rocky, in hand, their hobby got the better of them. Bobby put the dog down and he and Helen, unable to wait until they returned home, shot up heroin inside the bathroom on board. When they finished, they looked for the dog, but all Helen could do was run after him and scream as poor Rocky fell into the churning waters behind the ferry, another victim of drugs in *The Panic in Needle Park*.

Continue walking the same way and turn right on Broad Street. Cross to the far side of Water Street, then make a left on Water and a quick right on Whitehall Street. Head north until you reach Bowling Green and the front of the Customs House, which will be on your left.

25. Customs House. 1 Bowling Green. This building is now a museum, as it was in *Ghostbusters II*, when the spirit of evil emerged from a painting of Vigor, "the Scourge of Carpathia, the Sorrow of Moldavia," and declared that "now is the season of evil." Vigor commanded meek art

restorer Janosz Poha (Peter MacNicol) to find him a child so that he might live again. And Janosz almost gave him the child of Dana (Sigourney Weaver), on whom he had a crush, but luckily for Dana and the rest of New York, the Ghostbusters again saved the day.

Walk a few yards north to a spot on the curb to the right of the small plaza in front of the Customs House.

26. Whitehall Street across from Beaver Street. Northeast of the Customs House. They were doing their best to get along, which was not an easy feat, considering that one lived in the jungle of Manhattan and the other in an actual jungle on the other side of the world. After a heated argument that had Michael Cromwell (Tim Allen) chasing his son Mimi Siku (Sam

Huntington) through the streets of lower Manhattan, in *Jungle 2 Jungle*, they both stopped here and Michael taught his son how to hail a cab. In his view, a first step toward getting by in the jungle that is New York.

Return to the Customs House and facing it, turn to the right. Cross Broadway and enter Battery Park. Follow the paths and wend your way through the park until you reach the Soldier's War Monument. If you can't find it, ask a New Yorker to point it out: We're a friendly lot.

27. Battery Park. Soldier's War Monument. Movies about terrorism now seem both uncannily timely and horribly inappropriate but, like terrorism itself, they are a painful part of life. Two madmen came to New York and embarked upon a crime spree. They killed innocent people and filmed their torture and subsequent murder of Detective Eddie Flemming (Robert De Niro). With the help of a tabloid news show, their film footage even aired on television. But arson investigator Jordy Warsaw (Ed Burns) decided that their *15 Minutes* of fame had gone on 15 minutes too long. After a trial ended in a verdict of not guilty by reason of insanity, attorney Bruce Cutler (playing himself) led one of the killers, Emil (Karel Roden) through the crowd that had gathered here. But Jordy was in the crowd and knew which buttons to push. In response to Jordy's baiting, the killer revealed the truth. His 15 minutes, and his freedom, were up.

Continue through the Monument area, down the steps, and get a view of the Statue of Liberty, watching you from her perch in New York Harbor.

28. Statue of Liberty. She stands proudly, torch in hand, casting her light on the entryway to the

United States and the American way of life. Severely challenged by the terrorist attacks of September 11, 2001, attacks for which Miss Liberty had an unenviable front row seat, she continues to represent everything that is right about freedom. And imagine how a young Vito Corleone (Oreste Baldini) might have felt when he, though quarantined upon his arrival at Ellis Island, was able to gaze through the windows of his tiny room upon the Statue of Liberty, in *The Godfather Part II*.

Miss Liberty has made it into other films, but she hasn't always been treated with such reverence. In *Up the Sandbox*, a bored housewife, Margaret (Barbra Streisand) used to imagine her life being more exciting than it actually was. In one such fantasy sequence, Margaret and her cohorts sailed over to Liberty Island and pulled a caper inside the Statue, causing it to fall into New York Harbor.

Running from the cops, Mr. Fry (Norman Lloyd) climbed to the top, crawled outside and clung to the torch, and then his nemesis, Barry Kane (Robert Cummings) arrived. Despite the enmity between them, Barry did his best to save Fry, grabbing onto his sleeve and holding on for dear life. But then, in classic Hitchcockian fashion, the sleeve ripped away from the jacket, thread by thread, and Fry plunged to his death, with Barry holding onto nothing but the sleeve, in *Saboteur*.

And then the world came to an end. At least the world as we knew it. When astronaut Taylor (Charlton Heston) rode along the shoreline on horseback, he came upon one of the most frightening scenes ever to shudder the silver screen: Miss Liberty, or what was left of her, lying on the sand. For the *Planet of the Apes* was not somewhere out there at the far reaches of the galaxy, but it was here, on earth. And not just on earth, or in the United States, but really here, in New York. Armageddon had come somewhere along the line, and life as we had known it was over. Liberty was gone, too, with only a grisly reminder in the sand of what had once been and perhaps, would someday be again.

A chilling reminder of what Miss Liberty had to witness, on September 11, 2001, when Armageddon struck for real, and the towers of the World Trade Center crumpled by design of the devil's henchmen who continue to walk the earth.

Take a deep breath, let it out slowly, and scan the Hudson River for a tugboat. If you're lucky, you might see one sailing by.

29. Tugboat in New York Harbor. Of course, if you're really lucky, you might be able to see, and hopefully hear, Fanny Brice (Barbra Streisand) standing on the deck of the tugboat and belting out "Don't Rain on My Parade," in *Funny Girl*.

Tour 13

Something about tugboats must make people want to sing. In *Godspell*, from a tugboat, the happy-go-lucky group also belted out a song, this one about living in the light of the Lord.

Turn right, keeping Lady Liberty on your left, and walk north along the Admiral Dewey Promenade. When you reach Castle Clinton, work your way around it to the right and exit Battery Park on Battery Place. Head east on Battery Place, turn left on Greenwich Street and walk north until you reach Rector Street. Look to the northeast corner.

30. Rector Street and Greenwich Street. Northeast Corner. Although there isn't one here in real life, there was an ATM machine on this corner and it's where madman Patrick Bateman (Christian Bale) stopped for some cash after a hard day's work in the world of investment banking, in *American Psycho*. Sinking deeper into madness, Patrick was about to kill a stray cat, when a woman, a good Samaritan, tried to intervene. The cat was saved, but Patrick decided to shoot the woman instead.

In all likelihood, you will not be able to walk north any further on Greenwich Street for a long time to come. Looking straight ahead, there is an open space, significant not for what you see but rather for what you don't see. A gaping hole in the landscape, a chasm ripped into the fabric that is New York City. You will never again be able to get a good view, so the best thing to do is look again at the photograph at the start of this Walking Tour.

31. The World Trade Center. Twin Towers. In *Bait*, high up in one of the Towers, the personnel whose job it was to keep track of the whereabouts of Alvin Sanders (Jamie Foxx) were in place. A chip had been implanted in Alvin's cheek and they all watched to see if the man who had stolen $40 million in gold bars from the Federal Reserve and executed two bank guards in the process, would take the "bait" and try to locate Alvin. Before the operation got underway, Special Agent Ed (David Morse) gave the group a pep talk.

Jack Prescott (Jeff Bridges) knew that King Kong would eventually find the Towers, because they reminded him of a structure near his home, as they remind all New Yorkers of home. In *King Kong*, the great ape climbed the Towers, with the lovely and lithesome Dwan (Jessica Lange) in his grasp. As the army mobilized

below and whirlybirds circled above, Kong put Dwan down and nudged her to safety, choosing to face the machine guns himself. After such a display of gallantry, no one could blame Dwan for shedding tears when Kong fell to his death on the Plaza below.

Another location you may not be able to visit for some time is the Winter Garden, in the World Financial Center, across West Street from where the World Trade Center once proudly stood.

32. Winter Garden. World Financial Center. Marcus Graham (Eddie Murphy) was one of the last of the breed known as male chauvinist pigs. He thought his career had all but ended when he learned that his new boss was a woman. And it may have made matters worse that she wasn't just a woman, but a beautiful, sultry, sexy and smart woman, Jacqueline (Robin Givens). I, for one,

would love to have such a boss, but this isn't about me. At a gala event held in the Winter Garden, Marcus shared his concerns with Tyler (Martin Lawrence) and Gerard (David Alan Grier), colleagues of his and wondered whether he could continue to work for the company. But in *Boomerang*, Marcus would learn that what goes around comes around, and, for once, the chauvinistic shoe was on another's foot.

You have now reached the end of the final Walking Tour, **Walking Tour 13: America's Heart**, and the last of the 13 walking tours of *Manhattan on Film 2*. I hope you enjoyed taking the tours and will recommend them and this book to all of your relatives, friends, co-workers and people you pass on the street.

Movie Index